An Eclectic Gathering

by
Gerry Marcotte

PublishAmerica

Baltimore

First printing

ISBN: 1-4137-0611-8
PUBLISHED BY PUBLISHAMERICA, LLLP
www.publishamerica.com
Baltimore

Printed in the United States of America

Dedication

This book is dedicated to my two sons, Justin and Andre.
We've had our struggles and difficulties, for I've not always been
easy to live with, but I do love you both so very much.

In Memory Of
Cst. Ghislain Maurice, RCMP
1968-2003
You always respected me, as I you. Knowing I'll never see you
again leaves a void. You were one part of my many gatherings.
Salut, mon ami.

Acknowledgments

Thank you Rosie Desrosier for being so open and trusting, letting me feel comfortable about my works.

Thanks to Vi Sterling for being so honest in telling me that perhaps my writing was too personal for public display, yet indicating that the honesty and feelings moved her. The poems I've presented are very personal, but the ones you were indicating, I have them tucked away.

Thanks to Tammy. You needed a boost and you indicated some of my poems helped you. I hope my poetry may help others, too.

To Donna McWhinnie, thank you. Your professionalism, your understanding of the English language, your healthy comments, your suggestions I certainly did heed.

To Jamie Marks-Blahun…what can I say? You saw things in my poems that I had sensed and felt, but I couldn't quite put a handle on. You kept telling me my writing has so much feeling. Your nudging and prodding proved to be the catalyst that convinced me that I may have something to offer… Thank you so much.

Charles Goulet…God works through people, and you are an indication of this. Your encouragement, your critique, your contacts, your experience and knowledge as a writer, and your warm personality… made me feel I really had something worth looking at. Words cannot express my feelings of gratitude.

To all the people in my poems. In many ways, my life is the way it is because of your influences, and I thank you.

To my family—thanks. Some of the poems you saw me live through, saw me struggle, and saw me finally accept. Thank you for your encouragement. Each of you has been very special in my life, excellent teachers through emotions and feelings, things I've tried to instill in my poems. You have given me a lot of love…something I truly need.

Gerry Marcotte

Table of Contents

An Eclectic Gathering

I've often wondered what my goal is in this life…
Am I doing the right thing in my struggle to strive?
When my Creator calls, all my possessions will belong
to others. All that leaves is my soul. What may tag along
are my beliefs. Yet, they will have been left behind…
Contradictions? Yes, similar to my state of mind.

My ideas are assembled from many scatterings
of many impressions…an eclectic gathering.
So, what's my role? Of my words, some may avail,
of my opinions, others may feel that I failed…
All I ask of life is to give me the proper means
so that I may attain my task…to fulfill my dreams.

The Rooms

I am amazed at the capabilities of the mind: how it categorizes each individual and knows how much information to divulge to each one.

Therefore, I decided to try to write a poem about the mind based on individualism...who goes where and why.

The blueprint I ended up with was similar to the design of a house with its different rooms and what they represent in the framework of the house, the mind.

I enjoyed writing this...very interesting.

For those who wish...welcome to my rooms.

The Rooms

My mind, to a house it can be compared,
structured in sections, into different rooms.
To be at peace with my mind, I must know
whom to invite and to which room they're welcome.

The Living Room.
>   To this room, most people are welcomed here.
>   These folk, I don't let them get too near.
>   Superficial talk mixed with a beer.
>   A few laughs, even a few jokes we hear.
>   Nothing too serious, nothing to fear.

The Kids' Room.
>   This is the room where the children hang out.
>   A lot of noise, an occasional shout.
>   They're a part of me; so love I hand out,
>   by setting examples, by adding some clout.
>   I'll answer their questions to calm their doubts.

The Kitchen.
>   Here's where the family gathers to eat and talk.
>   Much debate is had. At times the walls rock.
>   Through all of this, many lessons are taught,
>   and, because of it, much advice is sought.
>   Feeding the body and soul, we learn "The Walk."

The Bed Room.
>   In this room, very few will enter,
>   for, to let someone in, I must be sure.
>   If married, my wife. If not, my lover.
>   Discussions and issues will occur.
>   This is where I open my chest of treasures.

The Den.
>A cozy, private little room for me,
>and a few close friends, who agree
>with my thinking, my philosophy.
>More often, though, it is my room to flee,
>to unlock the closets I want to see.

The Attic.
>Rarely is this far-reaching door opened,
>although I am welcomed like a long lost friend.
>Anyone else, the soul center will fend.
>In this room, there is no more pretend,
>for my inner secrets, these I must tend.

The Room of Mystery.
>No one enters this room. The price to pay
>would hardly be worth the pain, come what may.
>In this room, all mysteries are locked away.
>All the deep sorrows, hurts, and pains must stay.
>One day, if I must enter, to God I'll pray,
>for, I don't know where to start. I trust his way.

A Love Letter to Dad

Dad was dying of cancer at the University Hospital in Edmonton. As a family unit, we are very close. Therefore, those who could be at Dad's side during this tragic ordeal were there. We were so fortunate to have Aunt Lucille with us. We each took our turns being with Dad...day and night.

This particular night was mine to stay with Dad. When I got to his room, Dad was sleeping very peacefully. The whole setting was serene. The hushed voices of the nurses in the hall, the soft lights, and the antiseptic smell, even though I really don't like that smell, for there always seems to be sadness attached to it. Everything seemed to be in place. Actually, I felt quite spiritual, very mellow.

I got a pen and pad and composed a Love Letter to Dad. This was the hardest, yet most touching letter that I'd ever written. Many tears trickled down my cheek. How could I summarize my feelings concerning Dad in a lifetime of joy and pain, contentment and grief, happiness and sadness...LIFE!...LOVE!.... Actually this is/was an impossibility. One thing for sure, I really had a review of my life in relation to Dad. WOW!

This is the Love Letter I came up with. I truly do miss you Dad. I feel a lot of sadness for all the pain and sorrow I caused you, although I was very fortunate to have had a chance to make my amends to you before you passed on.

I do know I did give you some joy, happiness, and pride—to name a few emotions. Only now do I understand how much you really did love me, and equally how much you loved the rest. You had no favoritism. You were great!

Encore une fois merci. Je t'aime!

Ton fils,

Gerry

P.S.Dad died two days later...April 7/89. Father Doyle read this letter at his funeral.

A love letter to Dad

University Hospital,
Edmonton, Alberta.
April 5, 1989.

Dear Dad,

You are asleep now as you have been for the past few hours. Sitting here and watching you, I have a lot of empathy for your tiredness, realizing that your past 70 years were varied ones. The journey you chose formed many different paths, as the occasions arose. Your journey had sad moments, in fact, quite a few. Your losses of Mom and Claire are a few examples. You also had your fears, your resentments, for you are only human, but this journey has had a lot more compassion, love, understanding, and gratefulness. In my eyes, you have attained a great deal of serenity. You seem to have gained an inner peace through your conscious contact with God and having come to terms with yourself. It requires a lot of strength and courage to take one's personal inventory, plus to make amends and have no regrets. I sincerely hope I may attain this serenity someday.

I have to chuckle a bit thinking of the type of character you were. My God, everyone knew where they stood with you, like it or not. You were a very self-confident person. You were not afraid to admit to your mistakes; in addition, you were willing to learn from them. You were never a gossip nor a backstabber.

I could write so much, but I guess the real reason I'm writing this, Dad, is to say I love you so much, and I'll truly miss you. Through my faith, I have learned that upon your death you will enter a paradise named heaven. I should be so happy, yet I feel a lot of sadness. You brought and gave me so much security, so much strength.

Thank you Dad for having been such a good father, such a good provider, such a good support person, but most of all Dad, thank you for your love and forgiveness. You certainly gave me solid roots. You had a lot of difficulty letting go, to give me wings, but I understand the whys. You wanted only the best for me, and I thank you.

I am proud to be your son. I certainly have big footsteps to walk beside, for I could not nor would I want to try to fill your footprints, for they are yours.

Your time has come. There are no more so longs, Dad. What's left is GOOD-BYE! I hope and pray we meet again. God willing, we will. Pass on a good word to the Lord for me, Dad. I truly love you. May God bless and provide you well. Say hi to Mom and Claire...and to the rest of the clan.

Forever yours,
Your Son,
Gerry

The Sunset of a Horizon
(The funeral of a lonely man)

"To read skillfully the signs of grief, are an intricate part of, known only to the poor…or those of whom have suffered internally, externally, materialistically, or otherwise from an unfortunate mishap, and, have gained by it."

This is a little prose I wrote a while back. In this poem, I have tried to place myself in the eyes of Hans, an old German mishap I met on the Reperbahn in Hamburg. He sure didn't gain from my prose. Just to look at him, I could see the misery he had passed. Feeling sorry for him, I bought him a beer. At the end of the night, I was his friend. Actually, Hans' English wasn't bad, so with my little German, and his English, we made out quite well. Of course, the two bottles of cheap wine that we drank in his dilapidated room in Hamburg's slums sure helped.

Hans confided in me his life story. A lonely, lonely man he was. Hans told all that is stated to me other than his death, of course. I'm not sure if he is still alive, probably not. In my imagination, this is probably the type of funeral he had or will have. I'm sure it would be his sunset on a horizon, at the funeral of a lonely man.

The Sunset of a Horizon

(The funeral of a lonely man.)

A cold, somber December afternoon,
a single, lonely church bell rang.
Boots were crunching the snow in tune,
carrying a coffin. No one sang.

The journey began some sixty years ago.
Who knows? Nobody really remembers.
A childhood of much hardship and toil,
his mother died in his fourth September.
"The Plague," the old doctor did state,
had extinguished her life with a slow grip.
The Great War was on, so they dug a hole
and buried her, then began their long trip.

As the final 'Amen', the preacher said,
the cheap box was shut and sealed for good.
He'd found his happiness on this cold bed.
This seemed to be the only way he should,
for there was no other way that he could.

Somewhere down south, he finally left his dad.
He felt it was time to try his own luck.
A lot of searching with little success,
the beggars' line-up, he finally struck.
He'd hit the streets early each morning,
the same tattered clothes were his only dress.
Finally, a cheap laborer he became.
Times were very poor, with little rest.

Not very many people had come.
Only a few old friends that he had.
One or two even wept, and some,
deep down, felt they were a bit sad,
also, for him, they were a little glad.

She found him, one day, stone drunk,
lying on the sidewalk in a heap.
A beautiful woman she had been,
loving that loser, who was asleep.
She helped him off that dirty street,
and, for the rest of her life, he'd lean
on her, for she was his moral support.
For him, she was everything…his dream.

Outside—not far, a short distance walk,
the markings of the graveyard could be seen.
Some of the few people began to talk…
reminiscing…who and what he had been.

The highlight of his life was his marriage.
From that day on, it was all down hill.
Like before, the work was very scarce.
No money, and so many debts and bills.
Through dreams, they continued to exist.
One day, lying down to take a rest,
she died. Crying, kneeling beside her,
he held her tightly to his breast.

Getting closer to his wife's plot,
each of them displayed a silence.
Reaching out, they told her she must not
condemn him, to have much tolerance.
To be his guide, like she had done once.

The ebb was the death of his lovely wife.
Totally heartbroken, his life meant
nothing. Booze became his only true friend.
Further into the gutter his life went.
Finally, into an asylum he was sent.
Hallucinating, hoping it would end,
but no. Back to the streets he came,
to the slums. He didn't try to pretend.

The ground, frozen a dirty white,
the people, shivering beside the hole.
Darkness fell, leaving very little light.
The casket was lowered. Good-bye dear soul.

Hearing the laughter of some children,
out his grimy window he did look,
through sad, bleary, forlorn eyes.
In this cold room, his weak body shook.
Grabbing a cloak, out the door he went.
Near his door, letting out a deep sigh,
he crumbles on the sidewalk in a shudder.
Muttering his last words, the lonely man died.

The sunset, having faded away,
leaving no doubt of the night ahead.
The people hurriedly turned away.
Some, into their own thinking they fled,
the others, well, who could really say?

EPITAPH:
To poor people...Life is a dream.
To rich people...Life is a reality.
Please, be realistic in your dreams.

I'll Never Dream Alone

How can I write a poem trying to be you, my friend? I can't!

Therefore, I used a bit of empathy…trying to walk in your shoes…to attain some of your feelings. I know for sure that I've not completely succeeded, but I do know some of it is true.

We've become very good friends thanks to our fellowship. I have come to understand and respect you for the effort you've put in to reach and attain your physical, mental, emotional and spiritual well being, plus passing it on to others so they may attain this level. You really have come a long way this past year, in spite of all the obstacles placed before you. Congratulations!

In choosing this title, I chose to explore your past, for I need to understand the past before I can truly appreciate the now, and I sense you do too.

I feel there were many, many times in your past that you virtually were on your own…and it wasn't easy, trying to raise a young family with no support, always on the road from gig to gig. As a singer/ songwriter, I know you wrote and played about dreams…but that is what they were…dreams. Today, a number of your dreams are being fulfilled, and that's because you've shared them with others: friends, family, and especially, Jimmy.

Happy 1st Birthday, my friend. God willing and if you're willing, you'll celebrate many more. Thanks for your wisdom…I really do need it.

I'll Never Dream Alone

If I imagine something special, feeling it's out of my reach,
yet, not wanting to share this emotion with anyone…only myself,
it'll always remain a dream. But if I'm willing to breach
my thoughts, expressing my passions, unafraid to share the wealth,
then this dream will become reality. This gift is not mine to own
it's mine to partake…and to express gratitude for this loan.
If that is my choice, guaranteed…I'll never, ever dream alone.

Looking back over this past year, I'm amazed
at all the changes I've overcome, the different ways
I used to alter my life's picture… to portray…
and to feel self-love… to stop living in my maze.
I had to do something… too many tribulations,
too much hurt, not a whole lot of jubilation.
To live wholly, to have less pain… my situation
had to veer… for I had reached my termination.

Reflecting back over my past endeavors,
I honestly hope my life has changed forever.
For someone so smart, I wasn't too clever.
Going down my memory lane, I feel a shiver….

Jesus, I'm a nervous wreck! Please quit snowing…
and that bloody wind… it just keeps on a blowing.
I'll be shocked if anyone comes. They'll all need towing.
Finally! Neon! Nice to see the bar lights glowing.
Where's the back door? Holy cow! What a mess!
How will I get my equipment out? Strictly a guess.
Why do I love giving myself so much stress?
Why do I feel like I have something to prove…a test?

23

Walking into the bar, I sense my surroundings,
breathing in the atmosphere, gathering the folk's whim.
Ah shit! Here it comes again…that bloody pounding.
A friggin' headache… Ohhh… to stop that ringing.
Tension… that's all it is. Man! After all these years…
crappy roads, lousy venues, plus those damn fears.
Why in the hell didn't I choose a different career,
even though I know that it's me they've come to hear.

I wonder how the kids are. I'm sure they're fine.
Merely thinking about it, my gut knots up most times,
feeling guilt and apprehension… Phew! The signs…
feels like I committed a series of crimes.
I'd better stop these thoughts before they start.
Those damn mind games will tear me apart.
The physical pain feels like a thrown dart,
aimed at my emotional center… straight for the heart.

Surprise! The crowd's filling this joint up.
I've got to settle down… I'd better set-up.
I mustn't be too bad; I've been in worse dumps…
And who cares… just keep filling my cup.
I've come to hate the smell of cigarette smoke…
that stinky poison always makes me choke.
Towns don't change much… neither do their folks…
There's my friend, the rubby… he's always broke,
yet, manages to acquire his beer and 'toke'.

I guess I'll uncase and tune-up my guitar.
This stage is kinda neat… quite near to the bar.
It's rotund, and the speakers aren't too far,
and the lighting's good, certainly above par.
"MoonShine's Bar & Grill…Taste our White Lightnin'."
I like their saying! Gets lots of people yappin'…
I trust this night ole' guitar and me…my best friend…
will also get them talkin' about the music we're sendin'.

Hmm! What outfit should I wear tonight?
I think I'll wear the black pants and the white
turtleneck. Good mix with the black light.
My nerves are on edge. Why don't I feel right?
I need a good shot to settle me down.
"Put on my smile...get rid of that frown.
Let the folks think I like their little town.
Jees...! my mind's spinning round and round."

All right... Showtime! Let's get this gig into gear.
Those couple of shots made my head clear,
I feel good—give them what they've come to hear.
Maybe a few of them jocks'll bring me a beer.
People like my melodies in the songs I play...
they feel the music within my soul. Many say
they love this emotion, for I have something to say
not just something to show. Upon walking away,
I want to know that they're having a better day.

Snow's falling and drifting, I feel uptight.
I can't even see the road on dim or bright.
I'm gonna get me a room for the night...
and some medicine for my nerves... likely get tight.
Listening to the howlin' wind, I really feel alone...
alone and blue...scared and afraid of the unknown...
apprehensive of veracity and what's to be shown,
I take out my guitar and strum tunes that are known.

I love writing words and music...my feelings,
very therapeutic...a true process of healing.
My songs are like a poker game and dealing...
The hand tells it all, the cards are so revealing...
they guide my choice of action, my direction.
My tunes are usually written with lots of passion
because my life is filled with so much action.
What a hell of a road I chose! Feast or famine.

25

In imagining my life, my canvas…it's value,
I want to make sure my nuances flow true…
Yet, some background colors won't blend in hue,
and a few of the strokes…I don't have a clue.
I've come to realize with much apprehension,
that alcohol has a big role in this confusion.
I am a prisoner of my own misfortunes…
by choice…no wonder I have all this tension.

Yet, I'm not strong enough. I feel weak,
so, to booze I go…to give me strength, to seek
out my fate. The ending looks pretty bleak.
In all honesty, I think I'm up the creek.
Thinking about this makes me feel despondent,
because, in a negative way, I add much merit
to my belief of not being well, of being sick.
Luckily I know where to go for help, if I want it.

I'm extremely tired of all the schemes;
I need to go back and chase my dreams…
projecting my images on my minds screen,
enlarging them to actuality through my soul's beam.
The biggest change must be my sobriety,
and to do that I need a change of propensity,
followed closely by a dose of humility…
getting in tune with self and others…quietly.
Then…perhaps…my dreams will become reality!

The Renegade!

This poem wasn't meant to be, but here it is anyway. Unfortunately as such. Why do people, especially those I'd normally call friends, try to belittle me? I don't know.

It took me a long time to get the words down for this poem. Not so much because I didn't feel the verses, but because of my anger. I felt like a caged animal ready to fight back the only way I could... For the throat! I knew in my heart that this was not the correct way to handle the problem, so I let it settle down and tried to be calm about the situation.

I'll be the first to admit that my past has not always been a white sheet of paper. In fact, it's been blotched many times, and I can say I have a few regrets, yet why was I labeled "The Renegade"? I'm not sure how it all began. Is it their jealousy? Whatever their motive, it caused me a lot of resentment.

For those of you who have labeled me, I hope it never happens to you. If it does someday finally catch up to you, I can honestly say you deserve it. This is not said with any bitterness or resentment, yet when I look at it honestly, perhaps there is some of both those feelings still lingering in my mind... but that's my problem.

The Renegade!

As the man strummed his twelve-string guitar,
a tune, so mellow, so flowing, so true
escaped, slowly drifting to the stars,
filling me with a feeling I once knew.
Fingering the last chord, the sound did fade.
Smiling, he said, "That's called 'The Renegade'."

"Man has existed thru a past older
than tradition itself."

When Adam and Eve lusted in the garden,
resentment followed. God gave no pardon.
Through the centuries this has always existed,
gaining a few vices through all of it.
This sickness has no code of ethics.
People have their own personal mix,
using the tools needed...the brand and blade...
to blemish the one they call "The Renegade."

"The life time of man is so short,
why must we be so unhappy."

I awoke one morning truly 'pissed off'.
The rumors and gossip were more than enough.
My life was now a distorted adventure;
A few people had maligned certain chapters
to a fine degree of controlled vengeance,
making my life a misery...without chance.
Across my back these words were laid
in bold, bright letters..."The Renegade."

"It's not the man we admire or resent,
but the symbol of the man. We expect
more from symbolism than of the man."
All my life I've lived in a carefree style.
I've set foot in many places, traveled many miles.
To some folks I've become a symbol, a legend.
Because of this, they feel I must make amends.
I didn't ask anyone to live my type of life,
nor do I try to live theirs. Put away the knife.
Yet, they follow the very path I made,
and then brand me "The Renegade."

"For some people, searching for rainbows is their life.
The only thing…when the colors don't flow freely…
life for them becomes a misconception."

I've become a victim of my own character.
The garbage—the gossip they sought after—
created, to a few I love, ill feelings.
Today, the colors are a lot more concealing.
Circumstances have made it that way.
God has lent me Paulette, who now has a say
in my todays, and her I wouldn't trade.
She understands this guy called "The Renegade."

"Independence is not indifference, nor a lack of
communication. It's my ideas, my way to better
myself in my physical, mental, and spiritual quest."

Today, thanks to my love's understanding
of my distinct ways, I'm slowly finding
my independence, my total being.
All the shit I was hearing and seeing
leave fewer scars. I even feel compassionate
and warmth for these truly unfortunates.
Having made peace with myself, I have a spade.
Please, continue through your filth to wade.
I don't give a damn, call me "The Renegade."

As the man strummed his twelve-string guitar,
a tune so mellow, so flowing, so true
escaped, slowly drifting to the stars,
filling me with a feeling I once knew.
Fingering the last chord, the sound did fade.
Smiling, he said, "That's called 'The Renegade.'"

Outhouse Blues

Be it any time of the season, it doesn't matter, when you have to go to the bathroom, you have to go! I had the experience of using our famous outdoor toilets a few times. Some are okay, some are not okay, but it doesn't matter, when nature calls, good or bad, you go. In the summer time mosquitoes have a feast, and in the wintertime you freeze your butt. This particular poem is written about a winter experience.

Why did I write about outhouses? Hell, they are part of "The Cultural Heritage" of this country, and thinking about it is quite romantic, as long as you don't have to use them at all, and if you do, then not too often. But if you do have to use them often, well... after a period of time, you get those Outhouse Blues.

Outhouse Blues

When Mother Nature calls, you surely know.
Crunching a knee-high path through the snow.
Huffing and puffing, hot air ain't all you blow.
Fifty yards seems like a long ways to go.
Reaching your goal, you let out a long PHEW.
This is what they call the outhouse blues.

Stubbing your toe, you finally reach the bowl.
Pulling your pants down, you know it's damn cold.
This here's a deluxe model. It has three holes.
It even has a slope. Different sized poles.
It's a bitch in the spring, so near the slough.
Mosquitoes feast while you sing the outhouse blues.

On the floor near your feet, lies the ass-wipe.
In the far corner you see the lead pipe,
used as a crossbar to keep the door tight.
Grabbing a paper, you read the small type.
In the distance, you hear the old cow moo.
Her bells clanging to the outhouse blues.

From your throne, out the many cracks you peer.
Your ass is frozen stiff, so are your ears.
What the hell are you doing out here?
A cold wind blowing right up your rear.
It so damn cold, no doubt you'll get the flu.
This is what they call the outhouse blues.

Ripping the cover off a Readers Digest.
Of all the different kinds that's been tested,
it's still the best, it leaves a lot less mess.
So why take a chance, forget the rest.
Moving your cheeks, you know what to do...
wipe like hell, and yell the outhouse blues.

Pulling your pants up, you notice the sign:
"Help disease...and stink. Pour a little lime."
Walking bowlegged, you feel kinda fine,
even though you got a real sore behind.
Prince or pauper, it doesn't matter who,
always remember them ole outhouse blues

There Must be Something Wrong with Me

This fling lasted six months…if that. Donna had finally told me to take a hike, and I was feeling blue and sorry for myself. At this time, I was taking "Deutsch Lernen Klasse," and one of my fellow students was Sue, an American from Fresno, California. She loved to drink; I loved to drink so after classes we would go and "Schnaps Trinken."

She had a boyfriend back home, yet she got to like me a lot. I didn't care about too much, all I wanted was action and here was this good-looking gal liking my type of action. To be honest, it was exactly what I was looking for…no commitments, no responsibility. She was lonely, I was lonely…and booze was our crutch. I was caught up in the frenzy. Some time after, she started putting expectations into this "convenience." I wasn't willing to go that route; in addition, her boyfriend decided to come and visit. I told her I wanted out, and she left.

I was mad at myself for letting her go, for I was back in the same situation as before. I made it a point to keep in contact with her from time to time.

As I look back to this period…yes, perhaps there was some wrong in my feelings and actions. I'm not sure! Alcohol was my best friend, and still is. I love to drink, so why give up a good thing? Up to now, I haven't found anyone to replace this friend. Also, I want and wanted no obligations. I guess through a process of deduction I don't want anybody in my life that is looking for commitments. I like answering only to me. Yet, I know that sometimes I use people…and that bothers me a bit.

Why the poem? Well, Sue had many good qualities, of which honesty was a strong suit. That characteristic intrigued me, yet scared me. I want to see if I can understand her feelings by writing about them. I never totally succeeded, but I remembered a lot of other "good stuff," and wrote on that. Wherever you are Sue, thanks for "die gut amusieren"…for the good time. I think of you once in a while. Writing this poem brought back many memories…Thanks.

There Must be Something Wrong with Me...

I must be insane to want to dwell in all this pain,
yet, impressions of your loss photograph my brain.
That is so stupid, I'm the conductor of this train.
I choose the thoughts that I want; I have free rein.
For someone so smart, I do have short memory.
I really feel...There must be something wrong with me....

I truly sense a change in you, of course I know why.
I can't really blame you in wanting to say good-bye,
even though, you say, we can still be friends if we try.
Morals and mind games, I just want to lay down and cry.
You're willing to give it all up just to be with me.
I really feel...There must be something wrong with me....

When I reflect back to the happy times together,
I smile. I wish it could have continued forever.
Our frolicking fun, our little secret pleasures.
I'm not positive what kind of scale could measure
this joy, but it was superb. I want those memories.
Not too swift...There must be something wrong with me....

In remembering your happy smile, your gentle ways,
treating me with so much warmth, tenderness, and praise.
Wow! For the longest time you had me in a daze,
wondering what you saw in this bewildered maze.
I'm not sure what it was, but something caused a glee.
I really feel...There must be something wrong with me....

The one you are with now is such a lucky man.
He's so grateful, and he's one of your biggest fans.
You've stated that he's not your particular brand,
but, because of my decision, you took a stand,
and you made your investment. Nothing is for free.
I messed up…There must be something wrong with me….

I really loved your cleanliness and looks.
Your fragrance was that of a clear running brook,
fresh and inviting. It wasn't hard to got hooked…
and I did; yet, I resisted. That line I shook.
Why the fears, I don't know. Perhaps I need therapy.
I really feel…There must be something wrong with me….

You were never afraid to call a spade a spade.
What an asset. You never were much into charades.
Deception and pretend were never part of your trade.
If folks are honest, they don't have to hide in the shade.
At times, I felt you were my judge and my jury.
Was I right? Do you think there is something wrong with me?

When I saw you today, all smiles, you made my day.
I hardly see you anymore and I do worry.
I had to mention that I missed you a lot, and hey,
for me that's important. It's something I had to say,
a little refuel. I saw that my tank's on empty.
Why do I feel that there is something wrong with me?

Years have flown…and yet my mind photos are intact.
When my mind wanders off, it lets me know, in fact,
through memories, what a jerk…I could've had you back….

And Which Way Can I Turn?

After thinking about it for some time, I finally decided to make an attempt at writing poetry. This is something I've wanted to do for my own satisfaction.

I'm on my way to Europe…Life in Canada is at an end, for the moment anyway.

Looking back over my past, and trying to visualize my future, I'm just wondering which way I'll be turning, and, which way can I turn.

And Which Way Can I Turn?

Here I stand...
one great part of an era has passed.
I speak to my heart by moving my hand,
"Hey buddy! Why, why can't you make it last?"

And, which way can I turn?
Actually, there is only one way.
So tell me, which way can I turn?
Really, you should know the way...they say.

The era I talk of is many things,
for life is what you make of it.
Love, money, and many beautiful flings.
I can never get them together to all fit.

I have many debts, but no money,
for money is easier spent than made.
Physical appease can be bought, honey,
but your love sure wasn't. Now we must bade.

At twenty-three, they say, you're quite young,
Enjoy life, get out there and get groovin'.
Baby, I was taking you out for fun.
My time has come. Now I feel for movin'.

"Can't live with them" some continue to say.
I'll sure try, in my new life of travel.
"Can't live without them." Agreed, that's the way.
Man, who want too? More fun playing hell's bells.

I seem to know the way from what I feel,
so I guess it's my own destiny.
I hope you remember me, for I will
remember your many childish ways,
yet, grown-up desires and ecstasies.

And, which way can I turn?
Actually, there is only one way.
So tell me, which way can I turn?
Hey man, it seems you've found your way
don't let it get away...okay?

Here I stand...
One great part of an era has passed.
I speak...

I'm so Grateful for Having Flown with You

This poem is written strictly with you in mind. This past year has been pure hell for both of us, and now our relationship has come to its end. There are many things, issues, I don't understand, and perhaps I may never understand. My emotions have really been playing games with my mind, but I'm finally coming to terms with this. What you are doing is strictly your choice, and I, from these choices must make mine. You feel you are making the right decision, and if it's the right decision for you, then that's the way it should be. Time will let us know the true answer.

The word "freedom" comes to mind when I think of your new state of living. I'm sure you feel a sense of freedom, which is only to be expected. Never forget...to whatever type of freedom you choose, there is always a price tag...emotionally, physically, mentally, spiritually. That's life!

There were many good moments these past ten years for me, and I chose to be with you. For this time in my life, I'm so grateful for having flown with you. As my journey now takes me down new, exciting paths, this chapter in my life has come to a close.

Dear God, help us both.

I'm so Grateful for Having Flown with You

The moist fresh air exuberates me
as I slowly walk through the wet forest.
Feeling watched, I look up to the sky.
A beautiful eagle, totally free
circles above, protecting her nest.
I watch in splendor. How I wish I could fly.

> Before you, life was a chore. It was no fun.
> I had no purpose, no one direction.
> I was always on the move, on the run,
> wanting no commitments, simply action.
> I had almost lost contact with my soul.
> The alcohol was now in full control.

> Thank you, God, for having sent me you,
> a good and truly beautiful lady.
> I felt favored and lucky that's true,
> yet, frightened. I wanted to flee.
> Why? I was given what I had asked for,
> and in reality a whole lot more.

In the distance I hear her young ones' cry.
They are hungry. The mother spots below.
One diving swoop, the eagle has her prey.
Slowly, steadily, she attains her rise,
heads home to feed her young so they may grow.
Instinct has provided her the correct way.

I'm a recovering alcoholic,
today. Thanks to your will and fortitude...
You gave me a life...I was quite sick.
Still today, I must be alert of my moods.
Before God, before friends we signed our vows.
We have to live for today, for right now.

Paulette, you were everything I had wanted...
very good looking, nice figure, good morals.
You gave me a purpose to live, instead
of just existing. You made my world.
For the first time in my life, I felt peace.
Such a nice feeling. From famine to feast.

Ahead I notice a stump, so I sit.
In the solitude of space and time,
I imagine myself within the clouds.
Life is fantastic, a great relationship.
Everything I ever wanted was mine.
How I wish my emotions I could shroud.

The greatest gifts you ever gave to me
was the birth of our two beautiful sons.
I empathized your pain, your ecstasy.
I shall hoard and treasure these impressions,
these indescribable joys forever.
You were the vessel, God the creator.

I must be thankful for these miracles.
Justin, our first, a real good looker,
and a fine voice. He may become lyrical.
Andre' is a cute kid, that's for sure.
His feelings show by his dark piercing eyes.
One look will tell if you treated him nice.

The bubble burst as the sad thoughts crept in.
Down I come. Hearing the flutter of wings,
I, too, like the eagle must continue
my journey. Most engagements I do win.
This one I didn't, so off comes the ring,
even though I continue to love you.

    To be compatible, you really tried.
    I thank you for that. It must have been hard,
    pretending to take everything in stride,
    especially after being dealt the cards
    showing you that I was to be your ace.
    No future. You felt your life was a waste.

    It was beyond your ultimate powers,
    totally impossible to reciprocate.
    Everything I did for you turned sour.
    At times, during certain stages, I felt hate.
    I cried a lot. Much time was spent in a blur,
    and, why you feel this way, I'm not sure.

    You had many fears, so I gave you
    security, compassion, acceptance,
    warmth, stability, just to name a few,
    yet, total rejection. I had no chance.
    It's funny…what goes around, comes around.
    Even today, these feelings still can't be found.

Slowly standing up, my thoughts turn to her.
The great fun we had with a deck of cards.
How you would get so mad when I beat you.
It's the laughter I hope to remember.
The happy mem'ries of our house, our yard,
the quaint wood stove, the fern and how it grew.

I muse on our relationship
to no avail. It saddens me so.
I pray that God guides you on a safe trip.
Only you can ask. Only he will know.
Be honest in life, at least to self.
Have no regrets. Take care of yourself.

"Love isn't Love unless given away."
My emotions are truly fighting this.
I know the hour is near for me to say
my good-byes, and you I will truly miss.
You mean a lot to me, and yes, thank-you!
I'm so grateful for having flown with you.

In the distance, I sense the eagle flinch.
Her eaglets are beginning to squawk.
While she's gone, her young continue their cry.
Rays of sunshine ahead. I feel a twinge.
I'm nearing the end of my searching walk.
I have no regrets, I truly tried.

Thru My Eyes

This was a hard poem for me to write. The feelings were certainly there, yet, mostly the feelings of anger and loss of control... of both myself and the people in my life... were the most prevalent. There were many different things happening during this period, and most weren't good, at least, not good for me.

My former wife had come back, and this caused many problems. Andre moved in with his mother... and I really can't blame him. Justin, well, he went and lived with friends for a while. His life was in quite a turmoil, no thanks to me. Finally he left and moved away.

I love my sons with all my passions, yet in trying to show them the way things works for me, I get mad when they don't listen, and I push them away. I tend to forget that I'm not them, and they make sure I know it.

In this poem, I'm trying to see things as they really are, and perhaps through open-mindedness, I'll find some of the answers to getting my boys respect back. Dear God help me.

Thru My Eyes

To try to see it thru my eyes
You'll notice that I sometimes cry.
Am I seeking some sort of curry?
Or is it time I'm trying to buy
when you may find me on my knees?

> To love, then to lose, really what can I say?
> I want to lash out, to make someone pay,
> and yet, in most cases it was my voice
> that forced the special ones to go. Bad choice.
> and now, thinking about it makes my eyes moist.

To try to see it thru my eyes,
Resentment and anger lurk and hides.
A real bad combination for me.
While waiting for the other to die
I drink the poison with much glee.

> Well, I did lose my boys, and that really hurt.
> Because of my attitude the bubble burst.
> But really was it ALL my fault? I say NO!
> Wow, the flames of discord, they sure did grow.
> Why? Others needed to play the role of hero.

To try to see it thru my eyes
You'll see one I've come to despise.
I often wish I could just flee.
Naiveté may be my demise.
Man, it would be nice to be free.

I'm not responsible for others' actions,
but I do have a choice to sanction
if I feel they're heeding my script, my play.
But how can they know my thoughts or what to say?
They can't. Therefore, it becomes a real foray.

To try to see it thru my eyes
may prove to be a big surprise.
Your feelings on who I should be
may prove to be my disguise.
Open-mindedness…that's the key.

Is it wrong to set regulations and rules?
I think not! Why am I portrayed as the fool?
It may be true, but somewhere I missed the pun.
Actually, I've missed a lot with my sons,
mostly their respect. At times, they have none.

To try to see it thru my eyes
don't be afraid to dig and pry.
You may get a chance to see
how hard it is for me to strive,
and at what price, it costs… the fee.

I've experienced in love an urge to forgive.
Also, memories are loves best preservatives.
Why do I continue holding on to my kids?
Let them discover what Freud meant by his "ID,"
and "EGO." Ultimately all will fit.

To try to see it thru my eyes
how do you think I can survive?
Change of attitude it must be.
only then will I truly rise
to feel the sun, to see the trees.

The love I held back is the pain that followed,
and to think that I let myself go so low.
Happiness: a truly fragile emotion
that I want to keep in large proportions.
To do that I need the gift of good fortune
and to regain the love of my precious sons.

The Shattered Dream

I've wanted to write a poem on my feelings concerning my divorce for a long time. We have been divorced at least ten years, yet every day there is always something that reminds me of her existence... unfortunately.

She was the one who pulled the pin on this relationship. My insecurities took over. I really wanted her to stay even though I knew that she had never loved me. For her, this marriage should never have happened... therefore, it was really a false start. For me, I took my vows seriously; therefore, this ending was a terrible blow to my self-esteem.

For me, this was a death of a relationship; I had to go through the whole grieving process. I went through the denial stage, the anger stage, and the fear stage... to finally arrive at the acceptance stage. It took me a long time.

Through all of this, I had custody of our two boys. I gave it my best effort as the role model, but in all honesty, my role portrayed was not a good one. I've had many problems with my style of bringing up children. Every time I think of the idea of me trying to raise our sons, it gives me cause for anger. In a marriage, two parents have enough trouble raising kids, therefore, when it comes to me as a single parent with all these responsibilities, I get so mad at her for abandoning her part of these responsibilities. Because of her leaving, because of the type of person that I am, our children have been the biggest losers.

When we were going out, we had dreams. We imagined all sorts of neat scenarios. I was aware that many of these dreams wouldn't come about, but together we could create realistic goals. I was counting on our love for each other to pull us through the good and bad days, that we'd live a happy, contented life together. Was that a dream? Hindsight says yes. Well then, that was my dream, and when she walked out the door, she shattered my dream.

The Shattered Dream

"'Tis better to have loved and lost
Than never to have loved at all."—Alfred Tennyson

The Omega: The end!
Going through my divorce caused me so much stress.
Unlike physical death, where one has gained one's rest,
emotional death turns out to be an avenging mess.
So much was extracted, I felt violated, undressed,
complete total exposure… stripped to the flesh.
The lawyers were the only true winners of this test.

How do you say farewell to someone you dislike so much,
and yet had loved so intensely with impassioned touches?
Life has to be stimulating, not diminishing, as such.
In our alliance, we often needed a crutch…
things were not well. Our values were turned upside down.
To have goals without a plan is not very sound,
especially if there is no timelines to be found.
Just as well having none. Both ways we were sure to drown.

It took a long time to get here, but we finally made it.
To be honest, to come this far didn't take much wit.
I thought we'd both strive for the same intent, not quit.
I was working on a game plan, trying to make it fit.
I forgot…it takes two to play. One can't merely sit.
The lawyer took my check and handed me the writ.

Finally, we ended up by getting a divorce.
I felt guilty, I felt shivers down my pores,
and why, I'm not sure. She chose the course
we'd be following, without any kind of remorse.
She'd made the decision to start a new life,
and to do that, she chose not to be my wife.
Because of her "issues," we ended up in strife
over the kids. Our thoughts just didn't jive.

She sure didn't feel that I was the more stable,
and rightly so, even thought I received the label
Of "custodial parent." I didn't feel capable
in this role. For some strange reason the table
had turned. The truth be known, I wasn't so able.
Lessons to be taught... Raising kids is not a fable.

For single parents, I truly have a lot of empathy.
I know... I am one. Trying not to offend anybody,
I usually end up offending everybody....
I guess that's what happens on this journey.
I feel I was shafted, trying to do this on my own.
I found it to be more error than trial in our home,
no one to discuss with, therefore my way is chosen,
and my kids are the one's picked to be shown.

Through experience, I've learnt to keep
on plugging, in spite of the road being steep.
Whenever I feel sorrow, I must search deep
in my soul to find what provisions to seek,
for that which gave me joy, also makes me weep.
True strength lies in gentleness to be complete.

My character seems to love being caught in mire,
yet, there are so many things my heart desires.
When I think of my former, often my ire
surfaces. She was one that I use to admire.
Time has changed her. Much poison has crept.
So greedy, she takes without remembering, you bet,
but when she gives, she'll never let me forget.
The irony is… she still feels I owe her a debt.

In spite of having the children to protect and raise,
I've often caught myself staring, in a daze,
wondering the secret of her tangled thoughts, her maze.
I felt that often in our union there was too much haze,
too many shadows were cast… by me… by my ways.
She got tired of my antics and soon nothing fazed.

It is impossible to describe the love for a child,
at least it is for me. From the day of their arrival,
and for the rest of my life, their precious survival
I will defend…if they wish. Each has his own style.
I'm responsible for the effort, and that I accept,
but, not the outcome…therefore, there's no need to fret.
I realize there are many things they can expect,
yet, they also have obligations that must be met.

Through life's challenges and experiences,
I've learnt that if and when I use expedience
to achieve an end, I often become tense.
Through divorce, I really had to make some sense
of my shortcomings, things that've troubled me since
my beginning. My children must not walk these prints.

Years have passed. I guess I'm slow to learn,
yet I have finally figured out how to discern
a bit of insights. My love, they don't have to earn,
that I give, but my thoughts are mine to churn;
therefore, they have to figure out their own opinions.
Over much consideration, I made this decision:
"Kids... live for your future, not in my past impressions.
Reluctantly, I surrender this... this is not my fashion."

It would be so nice to be able to rewind,
to go back in time, and some how find
that illusive answer to this particular rhyme.
I've been this one parent family for some time,
and I hate it so much. There are so few guidelines
showing me how to create, for myself, space and time.

The Alpha: The Beginning
I remember the night you entered my scene.
I liked what I saw: beautiful, single, and clean.
We laughed and joked. Your whole presence gleamed.
I asked you out. I thought we'd make a great team.
Over time, I was proud to display you as my queen.
You lied about your love, leaving me with a shattered dream.

One night I had a dream that Dad was talking to me:
"Live in the moment...what's not yours to control...let it be.
Be gentle on yourself. Be grateful for what you receive.
Be accountable for your actions...Don't blame...please.
Be honest in all your endeavors...That is the key
to settling your past accounts with spouse...you'll see.
Divorce is...bringing to term, a closure actually,
letting two good people start anew...to be free!"

53

Had me a Talk Just the Other Day...

It's fun talking to old friends once in a while. Because of the pressures in society, I seem to have very little time to stop and relax, and make the effort to get in touch with friends and relatives.

In this poem, I have done just that. Most every person mentioned in this poem will only be remembered through memories. They have all passed away. Each and everyone was special in some way to me. I thank you all, and I enjoyed having me a talk with each one of you. It was just like old times...Today.

Had me a Talk
Just the Other Day...

Had me a talk just the other day…
with Freddy. He sure had a lot to say:
"Man, heaven is the greatest place ever.
You wish it, it's here. A real pleasure.
I see you have a charming woman there.
Charlene was special. You honestly cared,
but, not enough I guess. You needed change.
Boy! some of your choices were rather strange.
Continue the road you're on, you'll go far.
Keep a level head, friend, you ain't no star.
Hope to see you here at a future date.
If things go right, you shouldn't be too late."

Had me a talk just the other day…
with Ike. He sure had a lot to say:
"Hi buddy! When I think of Hay River,
the fun, the sadness…I feel a quiver.
I still play guitar and sing quite a bit.
Got me a super band. We's a big hit.
Our harmony…WOW! So precise, so clear,
and guess what? We don't even need a beer!
Talking of beer...Booze and drugs, my friend,
sapped me of my life. I just couldn't fend.
I left behind a lot of sad memories.
Take it from me, it ain't worth the fees."

Had me a talk just the other day…
With Benny. He sure had a lot to say:
"You've changed quite a bit since Sangudo.
We sure partied a lot. The booze did flow.
Stanley, Fred and me, we rap sometimes.
We're all buddies. Everything is just fine.
I was getting worried…your steady decline.
Crutches, that's all it is. Not worth the time.
Treat your woman with respect, asshole.
The gals you used before, most had no soul.
Got to know some of your friends. Nice people.
Sure surprising those you meet in the fold."

    "There's Peter, Paul, Joseph and James,
    Mathieu, Mark, Luke and John, too.
    Also, a lot of Mary's, Suzie's and Jane's.
    I'm learning the ropes from them. I'm quite new.
    My friends, they showed me how much I'd won,
    when God made His presence. He's number one.
    Anyway, enjoy life… have lots of fun.
    Eternity's forever… it's a long run."

Had me a talk just the other day…
with Mom. She sure had a lot to say:
"Hi Son, it's been a while since we've spoken.
I saw Eugene and I thought he was joking.
He said you'd finally quit drinking. Thank God!
The road you chose, the lessons you were taught,
I cringed. You seemed on some kind of a quest.
I'm proud of your changes. You've passed your test.
Paulette is soft spoken, yet she'll raise her voice,
if there is danger. You made a good choice.
She compliments you. Treat her with kindness.
With your sense of humor, not merely in jest."

Had me a talk just the other day...
with Dad. He sure had a lot to say:
"Thanks for the letter you wrote about me.
I'm so happy that you could finally see,
that I wasn't quite so dictatorial.
It bothered me so much when we quarreled.
I'm in constant contact with your Mom and Claire.
We sure do discuss our family affairs.
It's really to bad about you and Paulette.
Life's tough. We all thought she was a sure bet.
It's nice to hear you asking us for advice.
We'll help! So don't be afraid to shake those dice."

Had me a talk just the other day...
with Willy. He sure had a lot to say:
"Hey, little Frenchman! How's it going?
From up here, you seem to have grown,
which is nice. I see you still like to tease.
Humor is great, but change your jokes... please!"
Your friend Susan seems in total grace.
She's finally found her dwelling place.
She deserves it here. I know she'll do well.
Like you and me, she raised a little hell.
Mom and Dad say hi! They're up here with me.
To get through these gates, honesty is the key."

"You're starting to know a lot of people here:
    There's Peter, Paul, Joseph and James,
    Mathieu, Mark, Luke and John, too.
    Also, a lot of Mary's, Suzie's and Jane's.
    I learnt the ropes from them all. I am quite new.
    My friends, they showed me how much I'd won,
    when God made His presence. He's number one.
    Anyway, enjoy life... have lots of fun.
    Eternity's forever... it's a long run."

The Era: From Dawn to Dusk

This is a poem for Pépère Marcotte. Each of us can remember a specific time in your era that we can identify with. My specific time was when Uncle Louis Blanchette and Dad went to Saskatoon to pick up a pony for me, from you, Grandpa, the pony you had promised me as a child. His name was Trigger. He looked exactly like Roy Roger's Trigger, except, he was shorter. The joyful hours I spent with Trigger cannot be counted. I thank you for that joy as a child and adolescent.

In writing this poem for you, I have tried to portray your life from the beginning to today. It's very difficult to write a few verses for such a long period of time. This Era: From Dawn to Dusk, includes eighty-five years… 31,045 days.

Félicitation Pépère and Happy Birthday. I am so pleased to be part of this celebration.

Your Grandson,

The Era: From Dawn to Dusk

DAWN:

> The sun, starting its climb from the east,
> sends us the signals for the day to come.
> A long ways off, we hear the sounds of geese,
> searching for and finding that fertile pond.
> Their instincts guide them to and from.
> The start of a new day…Oh beautiful Dawn!

March 13, Oak Lake, Manitoba, 1896.
Anastasie gave birth while Adelard
waited. "Let's call him Ernest, just for kicks.
With that poker face, he'll be great at cards.
Who knows? Life may be good for him like us.
I guess it all depends on what he does."

MORNING:

> The sun slowly climbing higher and higher,
> the morning mist leisurely disappearing.
> Bees searching for that delicious cider.
> Some cumulus clouds in the distance nearing.
> New leaves, swaying on its branches with ease,
> indicating a slight refreshing breeze.

Prud'homme; A wild stallion…unbroken,
at the outset of the twentieth century,
is where the family had awoken.
A new home, new life. The past, they buried.
The parents were blessed with eight children.
Lots of hard work. Nature would not befriend.

At first sight, Ernest knew Rose was for him.
On a cold November morn, they married.
After many "ponces" of rye and gin,
their days together began. Grampa carried
his new bride to the threshold of their new home,
their farm. A young couple starting on their own.

There's a time for planting and for sowing.
The crops weren't great; still they had four children.
Times were poor. The harvest hardly growing.
Their kids grew up with Marcotte traditions.
Roland and Raymond were loud and determined.
Robert and Lucille were great persuaders.
Unique each one. They are well remembered.

AFTERNOON:
    The sun, having climbed to its peak by noon…
    now starts its decent towards the west.
    Someone in the shade is whistling a tune.
    This is his time of day to relax, to rest.
    Sounds from the playground of children playing,
    "I'm enjoying life," their laughter is saying.

Saskatoon…208 Avenue I North,
Grandpa bought a quaint little grocery store.
When someone walked in, they felt so much warmth.
There was always laughter and the odd roar.
Sadness struck the family. Grandma died.
After a lengthy illness, God was her guide

Grandma's departure left a great big void,
but, as life must go on, Grandpa's did also.
One day he was unequivocally joyed.
Winnie became part of our family flow.
She knew him, she loved him, she wanted him,
and together they chose to sink or swim.

EVENING:
Rabbit and gophers skirting in the field,
as the sun to the west shows its full force.
The wheat, blowing gently, shows off its yield.
Glancing east, a silhouette outlines a horse.
The sun, receding further, leaves no doubt.
This day is ending...the sun wants out.

With many card games and many old friends,
The Bell Block became their way of life.
As landlord and caretaker, there was no end.
Answers to problems he had to derive.
They made time for dancing and a glass of rum.
Hell, a man can't live without a bit of fun.

I'm a romanticist; I speak from the heart.
My emotions guide my thought pattern,
therefore, I know when and how to start
projecting love... something I had to learn.
This feeling inside cannot be bought.
No! It was something that Grandpa taught.
Thanks for showing me... it wasn't just talk.
In reality, I owe you for a whole lot.

DUSK:

Rocking back in his chair, man reviews his day.
The pro's, the con's, and what needs to be changed.
The sun is practically gone, merely a ray.
Shadows are lurking. Objects appear strange.
The moon starts its rise without any fuss.
The beautiful Era: From Dawn to Dusk.

The Play

A few weeks ago I was an actor in a production called *On ne badine pas avec l'amour*, a play by French Playwright, Alfred de Musset. Translated, the title means *Do not Trifle with Love.*

This was the first time since College Mathieu, Gravelbourg, Saskatchewan that I was in a production. That was some time back. I really enjoyed the role I had. I met many good people, smart people. It was a thriving experience.

In this poem I'm trying to reconstruct the amount of time, energy…Work…that went into this play, then to base it on an everyday situation. In other words, the production called "Life."

Bear with me…The Play has begun.

The Play

People on their feet yelling and clapping.
"Encore, Encore" was the sounds that we heard.
On the stage, we appear once more, laughing.
Bowing, we disappear. It's all over.

We've done what was asked: To perform.
For some, it was a difficult task,
while others portrayed their natural form
behind an imaginary mask.

To be honest about "Life," we're all actors,
of sorts. Some are better than others.
To play, we all have very distinct parts.
We choose our script. It comes from the heart.

Tonight's performance took a lot of time.
Pierre had to find his many characters.
With very much practice, we learnt our lines,
to become what was asked: To be actors.

Each of us had different roles to portray.
There were those who had the major roles.
These folk had much to learn, much to say,
about the image of another's soul.

In life, a few have prominent positions.
They try to influence our situations.
Most are knowledgeable, with much to say,
yet, some use dirty tactics in their play.

Then there are the secondary parts.
Very important factor of the play,
actually the essence. By heart
they learnt what they had to say.

In life, most of us have a small script
in a big production. We're the labor force,
and if we really wish to make our big hit,
we must know where to find our resources.

From the beginning to the very end,
we rehearsed the character's thoughts, ideas.
As actors, we were taught how to pretend,
to escape, to make believe we had no flaws.

In life, most of us wish to be someone else,
at least for a while, so we fantasize.
To do this, we put ourselves on a shelf,
and pretend this new look, our disguise.

Finally, we arrive at the big night.
We are all nervous, everyone is tense.
Our imagination leads us to fright,
leaving us with no direction, no sense.

Make-up, lights, Kleenex and mirrors,
are a few of the crutches used constantly,
to mold the personage, to gather our fears
of doubt, and to help store them away.

In life, many of us utilize crutches,
to hide our feelings, our desires.
But this is an escape, we lose touch.
Inadvertently, we become deniers.

A sense of relief was felt by all.
It's over. Back to the routine again.
Getting into that groove once more, is no ball.
To face reality is not the trend.

In life, we breathe a sigh of relief,
once in a while, for a job well done.
It was really worth it, and not much grief.
Isn't that great? Sometimes we have some fun.

This play exemplified many things
about life. How to strive, how to survive
using the right tools, pulling the right strings.
To listen, then action, are both very wise.

The Play: Life! The Stage: Your Surroundings!
The Actors: Each one of us! "Break a leg!"

How Do I feel?

I needed to talk to someone, not just in bits and pieces here and there. I met this therapist and we proceeded to talk. In our conversation, I mentioned that I like to write poetry. She said she'd like to see some of my poems; in addition, if I wanted to write my feelings, she'd be happy to read it.

When I sat down, and before I began writing, I asked myself: "How do I feel?" My very first reaction to that question was "I love Christmas!" I'm not sure where that came from, but I felt compelled to write one verse...eight lines..."I do love Christmas!" I guess I'd been thinking and spewing so much negativity, that my mind just rebelled and wanted something positive and to project something that I really love...Christmas!

That's the reason for this poem, but I must say I did really enjoy getting back into it. After having not written in some time, how would I gauge this poem? What the hell do I know? That's just how I feel.

67

How do I feel?

How do I feel? This is how I feel!
I feel abused, I feel truly used.
I have a lot of anger and resentment,
therefore, to fully comprehend, I must muse
instead of always re-acting in haste.
But, it's hard, for some near to me use tricks, a ruse.

How can I change?
Well, I've come to realize that certain trends
don't change, come what may. If I do the right thing,
no doubt, things tend to come out right in the end.
Who do I control? Me! I must do it right!
Then follows the where, what, why and the when.

How can I change?
Life has taught me to face issues as they are…
not excuses. I can live with my failures,
I mean the door to my humanness is ajar,
but, I can't nor will I live with the reasons
that take away my right to fail, to falter.

How can I change?
One thing that's taking me a long time to learn
is changing directions, changing thought patterns.
If I proceed down the same path, making no turns,
it's guaranteed I'll reach my destination,
but, the result of this choice is a real concern.

How can I change?
In true perspective, I look at my lifestyle.
Trying to be honest with my options
I realize, at times, I can be quite guile,
deceitful...justifying my controlling ways.
All I end up with is a pile of bile.

How can I change?
There's no congruence in my life today.
Actually, I'm a walking contradiction,
pliable and flexible, like a mold of clay.
I must search and research. I must be honest.
Easier said than done. I tend to stray.

What's the answer?
I'd like to say I don't know; yet, I do know.
God's gift is my life. My gift is how I live it.
Why must I always cause waves, not go with the flow?
Listen to my thoughts. Act instead of react.
Follow my conscience. Plant good seed, use my hoe.
For others to reap, I must have something to show.

Is this really the answer?
It sounds good, even has some rhyme to it,
but, really today, how do I feel?
I don't know!
Maybe it's just a north wind a blow....

The One Day Child

In a society like ours, which, in many cases, has very little time for its children, I've often wondered how these children feel.

I tried to place myself in the mind of a child that has become a survivor because of the living conditions they are brought up in. It's impossible for me to even try to understand this sickness, for I wasn't brought up in such an environment. Because of other people's experiences, and my awareness, I certainly have gained a lot of empathy; therefore, I am trying to imagine what it's like to be a One Day Child.

Many of these youth, the ones that are in the family environment, are beaten and shoved aside. They did nothing but to be born to receive this kind of treatment. I don't have to wonder why there is so much hate and crime amongst our youth, and I don't have to dig too deep to find the biggest part of this problem—the parents!

My sister Lillian is now working in a group home for youth. Her job is to try to break the barriers of the more fortunate kids who are put in this home. She shows these children that life is more than hate and destruction, that life is more than one day, that there are many good days filled with love, hope, and security. I have a great admiration for Lillian, to want to help these beautiful children. Unfortunately, some kids don't make it.

I would like to thank Billy, wherever he is today. To have had the opportunity to meet him and to have seen his lifestyle… well, he's the reason for this poem's existence.

The One Day Child

His eyes have turned a misty red,
His tears are beginning to dry.
Out of some corner he comes,
where he has, again, sat and cried.
    The lonely One Day Child.

He has shed many tears today,
of loneliness and asking: "Why?"
His body has no warmth in him,
for his heart has shaped into ice.
    The lonely One Day Child.

To unwanting parents he was born,
a child that was a mistake.
They ignore and push him aside.
He learns the system, he learns to take.
    The lonely One Day Child.

He feels so much fear in him,
yet, wants and desires much love.
Never smiles… always afraid.
Today, is it the fist or the shove?
    The lonely One Day Child.

Everyday is a hell on earth,
yesterday's worries…tomorrow's fears.
Each new day, more than the last,
he magnifies it through stained tears.
    The lonely One Day Child.

His soul becomes a torture test,
hoping that soon it will end.
He's heard of God and the angels,
but, a hand they don't seem to lend.
  The lonely One Day Child.

His young mind so warped with hate,
he cries out, wanting to avenge.
Through muffled tears that no one hears
he plans, he seeks out his revenge.
  The lonely One Day Child.

This youth, like so many others,
tries to live one day at a time.
He's looking and hoping to find
someone who is somewhat kind,
perhaps one who'll listen and care.
But, in the world of this child,
life's a struggle, nobody cares.
Each new day is another trial.
  The lonely One Day Child.

Yesterday's Youth...Today

Old cronies, Golden age, Old folks. These are just a few of the names we use to distinguish our senior citizens, people of whom we should be proud.

In this poem, I let my imagination take over and try to feel what our fathers and mothers, our forefathers and foremothers feel today, and what their feelings were in years gone by.

My personal thoughts are that I hope to gain the respect of my peers, as well as that of the younger generation. I truly respect and appreciate our seniors.

Thank you, yesterday's youth, for my today. Without you, I would never be here today; therefore, this poem wouldn't be written.

I want to thank two particular people as guides for this poem...Grandpa Marcotte, and Grandma Lemire. I was lucky to have had them in my life.

Yesterday's Youth ... Today

In trying to visualize old age,
I look around, and frankly ask myself:
"Where and when does old age truly start?
I guess it must have to come from the heart,
to feel this loss of active vital wealth
in one's body, in one's soul of one's self."

Of course, there's the odd one that is ageless...
physically, mentally, and spiritually.
It is so beautiful to sit and talk
with these elders, or take a small walk,
experiencing their constant energy,
yet, tasting their wisdom dished out for free.

For most, their youth was only yesterday,
so it seems, at least in their own minds.
To sit and listen to them talk of the past,
I'd think: "It seems like the day before last!"
When the mind discloses touching stories,
the play back is of wonderful memories.

Then there are some it's just a fantasy,
of which they have no choice but to believe.
Observing these truly unfortunates,
deep down in their soul they know it's a trap,
but there is no escaping, so they play,
choosing whomever they want to portray.

For others, it's the dreaded sickness.
The mind functions very well indeed,
but the body is of such little use.
To top that, some of their children abuse.
So sad…nowhere to turn…total despair,
and, they end up in an Extended Care.

Women live longer than men do, usually.
Are women more able to handle stress?
Are men too headstrong, once out of the womb?
Women's perceptions are much more in tune
with life. Most females show compassion,
while most males show their contention.

When their final days have come, most elders
are in harmony with their Higher Power.
Of course, there are exceptions to the rule.
There are some that are truly fearful.
What will happen? They don't believe in heaven,
plus, really afraid of hell… and it's the end.

We are so lucky… we will always have
yesterday's youth, today. We must thank them,
we must give them the respect that is due.
One day soon, we will be yesterday's youth,
therefore, we should be using their wisdom
to pass on our knowledge to our young ones,
then, they do the same… and life continues on.

Don't Forget to Smell the Roses!

What a coincidence! I started writing this poem about a week ago, on happenings in my past, looking for changes, and, hopefully, finding less stress in my life. Last night I heard that my good friend Joe had died yesterday afternoon.

In many ways, Joe has been part of my continued sobriety for quite a few years. Joe helped many different people over the years in so many varied ways, yet, I wonder how much he really helped himself? I know I'm not supposed to take someone else's inventory, yet, over the years, I couldn't help noticing how Joe would encourage newcomers, how he would offer so much wisdom and advice, be concerned when things weren't right... a real caring, loving person... yet he always gave the impression that he felt he had so little to offer. What a fallacy! If only you knew how much of an impact you really did have on people, Joe. Again, I'm speaking for others, and I can't do that, I can only speak for myself... well Joe, you made a significant difference in my life, and I thank you many times over.

Joe's death gave me a chance to reflect on many issues from my past, at how invincible I thought I was, how much I took and forgot to bring back... without remorse or caring, how I really have changed in so many ways... good changes, yet I can go back to my past destructive thinking in a blink of an eye. What a paradox!

Joe, my friend, your death gave me a jolt. Before I reach that final stage, I had better start enjoying more of what's been placed before me, instead of always asking why these particular issues have been placed before me. In other words, to follow the current instead of always going against it, to enjoy living, to enjoy life... and make it a point to not forget to smell the roses.

Joe! May God bless and keep you well. I'll always remember your laughter, your different expressions... the way you'd describe things, your dedication... but the thing I'll remember most about you, Joe, was your love of people. What a quality to leave behind... so I won't forget, and what a quality your soul has taken, to your place in eternal life. Get in touch with my dad and all your buddies from the program. Without a doubt, it'll be one "heaven" of a meeting. Thanks, my friend. I really am going to miss you.

Don't Forget to Smell the Roses!

Being so caught up in my little world,
life is passing me by very quickly,
or so it seems. My mind plays 'mind games',
pretending that the past was not long ago,
or at least some of it, and that is true.
The so called "memorable events,"
the ones that keep popping up out of the blue,
most happened quite some time, already.
My stock is still replenished even though
I seem to be living off old mem'ries.
I wonder why I'm yearning for the past?
The coulda, shoulda, woulda's are no longer.

There was a time when every day was
a fresh adventure, an experience.
It was exciting, yet somewhat scary.
New people seemed to like my style.
Of course, some did not last too long,
while others stuck around for quite a while.
The odd one is still in my life today,
to remind me of "the good ole times."
These few left, continue to teach me
that, as good as I seem to think my past was,
I saw it through dark colored glasses.
Deceiving and "bull shit"… they're so right!

As I reflect back to those "fine times,"
there are some I vaguely remember,
yet, there is a lot that I've lost,
thanks to my past boozing lifestyle.
Realistically… how can I know
where I am or where I'm heading for,
if, in my mind, I don't know where
I came from or where I've been?
I guess, life is what's happening
while I'm making all those other plans.
In some ways that is still happening…
but less. I try to live for today… most times.

I used to get so mad and frustrated
when some folks would try to live my life.
No one can tell me how to live my life…
how can they? They don't know the secrets
of my heart, the "stuff" that makes me tick.
Yet, I play that game called "Control"
most everyday, then wonder why people
get choked-up at me. A real paradox!
I have to learn to live right now, this moment,
that the only one I can control is me.
Also, be thankful for what I do receive,
and, to be a lot gentler on myself.

To understand how much I've accomplished
in my life… good or bad… I must look back,
and appreciate the significance
of my dips and weaves, my ups and downs.
Only with the powers of perception
and conception can I know where I'm heading.
To attain this, I need the power of choice,
which is one of God's greatest gifts.
Imagine! I get to choose my destiny!
Thanks God for this cherished offering.
To learn from my errors, I must listen.
All the answers I need are inside me.

I often thought of myself as being
compared to a wild, uncultured rose.
Similar to a prick with an attitude,
and when my defenses were challenged
watch out! I became a porcupine.
Yet, when I wanted to, I was a nice guy
and some folks enjoyed being around me.
As I look over my past, in retrospect,
I notice that I've missed a lot of things,
by choice, unfortunately. But that's life…
and before I reach another aspect
of living…that being death, I'd better
learn to appreciate more my surroundings,
and…really take the time to smell the roses.

The Serenity Prayer

Why do I write a poem on the Serenity Prayer?
It's such a beautiful prayer. When I try and live up to my understanding of this prayer, I often feel tranquility, calmness, a feeling of being in tune with my Higher Power. In other words, I feel quite serene, and I love it. If only I could live this way always, or at least a good part of the time, for this prayer is life at it's fullest.

However, life being such an encompassment, I have a hard time with the crests and the ebbs. To go the full circle, there is much for me to accomplish. I figure attitude, that emotional feeling on how to perceive life, has a major role in attaining this. I try to be optimistic most of the time, though it certainly can and is a tough thing to do.

By writing this poem, it gives me one more glimpse at some of my defects of character. In other words, it makes me aware of where I must work harder to gain grounds on this fleeting Serenity.

"God grant me the Serenity…
to accept the things that I cannot change,
the courage to change the things I can,
and the wisdom to know the difference."

The Serenity Prayer

"God, grant me the Serenity…"

How I wish I had that tranquility,
that feeling of some conformity,
to be in control of my sanity.
At times, it seems, this ability
to express feelings of humility
I do possess. But then vanity,
that useless pride, becomes reality.

"To accept the things that I cannot change."

I sure have trouble with this… strange!
It seems I like things to be deranged,
then, I can feel worthy and rearrange.
Often, this causes resentments and rage.
People usually like to arrange
their own life styles, their own range.
Why, I like to decide my own change.

"The courage to change the things I can,"

I hate change, for it scares me to no end.
Similar to a box… I try to withstand
pressures from both sides, yet take a stand.
I like it when I can walk hand in hand
with my conscience, that voice that demands,
and feel good knowing I'm in command.
But not through force, merely a humble man.

"And the wisdom to know the difference."

Wisdom being: Knowledge, insight, and prudence.
Such powerful words making no pretense.
To be able to discern and make sense
of my feelings, yet to take a stance
without being harsh. No need for vengeance.
Plus, we mustn't forget the reverence
and the thanks due today, from this day hence.

I Had a Dream and it Slipped Away…

To write a poem on dreaming, I found very interesting. A person has many different types of dreams. I base this dream on love, be it unsatisfactory or satisfactory, and what feelings, reactions, and consequences are experienced in both instances.

When I fail to dream, I deny myself the greatest and the best parts… excitement and anticipation. Also, of the dreams that I remember, it's very stimulating trying to recall all the details, although once in a while I wish that I hadn't remembered.

Thanks to many lovely ladies for giving me the opportunity to be able to express my dreams.

Of the dreams I don't recall or remember, all I can say is:

"I had a dream and it slipped away…"

I Had a Dream and it Slipped Away...

To dream; Emotions and images,
so vivid, reflecting off the mirror
of the mind, leaving imprints on its pages,
to be stored, and yet so very near.
Most are dear, but the odd one does bring fears,
reliving sadness, liberating a few tears.

In the far distance, I could see her wave.
Abruptly, she turned and disappeared.
Time had come. There was nothing left to save.
In my dream, things I didn't want to hear
she told me. I questioned, in spite of her tears.
I had to know. Was she honest? Was she clear?

The images sent forth gave me some clues.
She was lonely, yet at times she felt glad.
What a paradox! My mind's pictures strewn,
scattered about. I felt betrayed, yet sad.
When I asked her to stay, she just laughed.
She didn't love me, but was that so bad?

I couldn't accept what she was saying.
Totally beyond my comprehension,
yet, in my dream, I began weighing
my options, researching many suggestions.
Gaining insight, I felt some compassion.
Maybe she's right! I started to ration.

I felt time, the true narcotic for pain,
would eventually attain its limit.
In my dream, I was calling her name,
asking her when she could come and sit.
Hell, life was too short, why not a visit?
To remain friends required no permit.

Will this dream continue on tomorrow night?
Who's to say…?
Perhaps I'll have completely different dreams…
and they may slip away…

But of the good dreams, very much pleasure
is brought forth, leaving me so content.
Descriptions of feelings as they occur
are recalled instantly of each event,
as I relive these to the extent
I choose. That's the way it was meant.

In my dream, I could almost touch her.
A beautiful woman, calmly serene.
So lovely. She was the one I preferred.
Quietly eager, yet so very keen.
Dressed to kill, wearing fashionable jeans
and a stunning top. I imagined that scene.

Walking towards me, we met and kissed.
Holding hands, we slowly strolled down the trail.
Hugging her, I whispered how much she was missed.
Reaching the lake, we noticed a boat in sail,
swaying from side to side. So, so frail…
a recall of past memories that had failed.

The secret of happiness is freedom,
and, the secret of freedom is courage.
To find courage, from the heart it had to come.
The nemesis of happiness and knowledge,
is fear. Together, a battle we waged,
to restore our love. We'd come of age.

She snuggled in close, I held her tight.
Our body curvatures molded like clay.
Yah! Everything was going to be all right.
I kissed her long... this image began to fade...
I lingered on, hoping that picture would stay,
but no, day had arrived. The dream slipped away...

I hope that this dream will return tonight.
Who's to say...?
Perhaps this night I won't remember, and...
I had a dream and it slipped away...

Love Will Not Fade Away

Dr. James Dobson wrote: "What wives wish their husbands knew about women." I quote Dr. Dobson: "You don't marry the person you think you can live with; Marry the person you think you can't live without." Well, Paulette, my decision is that I love you enough and that I don't want to live without you.

I'm certainly not always right, often, in fact, I'm wrong in my decision-making, but the thing is that I'm trying to make it better for us. One thing that is certain, today, my love will not fade away. This poem is about us. I love you.

Love Will Not Fade Away

Life can't give me joy and peace,
this is something I must face.
Life just gives me time and space.
Everything else I may lease,
including love, but come what may,
my love will not fade away.

Love has many descriptive nouns
portraying that special someone.
Tenderness, desire, affection
are but a few that maybe found.
But, once I've made my commitment,
that chosen love will be my rent.

After the gorgeous wedding day,
realities begin to set in.
Both of us is trying to win,
to change the other, come what may.
But, before long, we learn to respect.
It's a must for both, what the heck.

The right to criticize a loved one.
even if advice is constructive,
must be earned to be effective.
Lots of respect and devotion,
plus, have my house in order first.
If not, broken windows I can't curse.

Happiness is conditional.
I choose the state I wish to be in.
With you as my love, I can begin
enjoying life, and that's not all,
we can also enjoy our children.
It's amazing the love they send.

One truly beautiful form of love
is through our conjugal rights.
The mood, caused by music and lights,
is fantastic for making love.
The foreplay creates the desire...
Now, there's no stopping the fire!

Very soon, we will start looking back,
realizing one mem'ry at a time,
as the years, their toll they will find.
By this time, we should have the knack
of knowing each other quite well.
I sure hope there's still the odd yell.

Life, our final outcome is death.
No one...No one gets out of it alive.
Whoever of the two is first, my wife,
I guess, all we can do is really guess.
I will love you past that very day,
for, my love for you will not fade away.

Life can't give me joy and peace,
this is something I must face.
Life just gives me time and space.
Everything else I may lease,
including love, but come what may,
my love will not fade away.

Time Unlimited in the Rain

An experience while hitchhiking from Calais to Paris, France. I had gone to Calais with Andy, an Irishman from Belfast, whom I'd met in Paris. He had convinced me to go to Manchester, England with him. He said he'd find me a job in some pub. Of course, we had been drinking, and I wasn't hard to convince in that state of mind. By the time we reached Calais, I was sober enough to realize how stupid this idea really was, so we split. I was damn near broke, no job, but I still had my return plane ticket to Edmonton. So, I decided to head back to Paris.

I left Calais quite late, and it had started to rain while I was having a bite to eat under a tree. This was decision time... what to do, or really where to go.

Hitchhiking is good, but a man needs patience. I'm always thinking, but that particular night, because of the rain, I was lonely and these are the thoughts I felt.

I recall this night so vividly, like it was yesterday.

Time Unlimited in the Rain

Sitting under a tree,
just a little ole' me.
It's raining hard. Man it's cold.
The thoughts of my past,
like the day before last,
are blitzing through my soul.
-Time unlimited in the rain.

Once it was Hamburg,
then it was Gravelbourg,
Paris somewhere in between.
The memories are good,
as most memories should,
tho' the times were lean.
-Time unlimited in the rain.

Linda flashes through
on a note of blue,
like a broken record in 'C.'
Then, Irene and Jude
somehow intrude,
like it was all planned to be.
-Time unlimited in the rain.

Lightning's flashing,
thunder's clapping,
I decided to move on.
Coat tucked real tight,
thumb posted upright,
man I wish I was bombed.
-Time unlimited in the rain.

Light's piercing in the mist.
Car passes...hardly missed.
"Patience man," but I swore.
North Battleford appears,
so do Dodie and the Speers
and my mother of no more.
-Time unlimited in the rain.

I wonder where Freddy is
on a miserable night like this.
Perhaps he's protecting me.
A car pulls up on a splash.
Man, maybe I can crash,
if he's going the same as me.
-Time unlimited in the rain.

Again tonight it's raining,
and I feel that it's saying:
"You know, those were good times."
No doubt my little friends
of the messages you do send.
Yes, those were good times,
and, Time is unlimited in the rain.

My Love Won't Bend Any Further

This poem was a gathering of thoughts, images, and experiences from my own relationships and of others... friends, people who touched my life in some way. Some of these couples are still together today. I presume they felt that their love was important enough to save, and, by trial and error they stumbled through their petty differences to attain something they both felt comfortable with... and wish to continue to enhance their love. The big problems, in most marriages, seem to be fairly easy to deal with... it's the small, irritable problems that cause the most grief, and more often than not, is the main cause for separation and divorce.

Of the ones that aren't together anymore, some have begun new relationships, hoping things will be better this time around. If they leave the garbage of their last relationship at the gate of that closure, there's a good chance it'll work. Of course, there are others who have chosen to remain single... and the reasons vary.

I thank Jamie for the title of this poem. We were discussing many issues, and something she said, or the wording she used just clicked in my mind, and this is the result.

In whatever love bonding you are in... be it spouse, children, parents, friends... may your love be on a horizontal level, not a vertical level... so that your love won't bend any further.

PS. I had to try out my androgynous side, writing from the point of view of a woman.

My Love Won't Bend Any Further

You are the most amazing guy that I know,
even though, at times, your head is in the sand,
and, because of emotions, you won't pull it out.
If I mention anything, you commence to pout,
I'm not sure why! I love you... I'm your greatest fan,
and when we want, we put on a mighty fine show.
When our lives are in tune, we are amazing,
when not... it seems that time is just a wasting.

I ask you to stop taking my inventory,
yet, I turn around and ask if I've failed.
I thought I was my own person... Not true....
What kind of control have I given you?
I needed help, so... I left you a trail...
to see if you were interested in my story.
Why did you take advantage of my weaknesses,
my vulnerability and leave me with so much stress?

Caught between a rock and a hard place,
there is very little room to maneuver.
Why would love leave such an awful taste,
ruining our relationship? What a waste!
My emotions tell me: "This is forever!"
yet, my mind knows different. I quiver...
knowing my love won't bend any further.

I am so sorry I can't meet your standards
concerning some very important issues.
I really have tried, but to no avail.
Words don't express my thoughts very well...
I know, for I've left you a lot of clues,
though, I notice you seem to put up your guard
from time to time. I guess you've stumbled
on a few. Don't become Cain... I'm not Abel.

I hear your voice a whispering in my ear,
and, what I detect is a lot more denial.
I'm sorry! I truly can't help how I feel.
I need your support, not a bunch of deals.
Now it's your turn to walk the extra mile,
for, I've traveled a long ways just to be near.
Darling... open communication to your heart.
Show me some feelings, like you did at the start.

I want to try to be as honest as I can,
yet, our definitions are quite different.
You try to justify, where I look at the facts,
affecting me and you, wondering where the tracks
will take us if we don't keep up our rent,
our vows. Perhaps they will crumble to sand!
We have to be accountable... no more blame,
or, you know what? Say goodbye to our flame.

Most of the problems in our relationship
resolves around love! Why can't the solutions
also resolve around love? I'm game for that!
Between the two of us, we know where it's at.
I'm really not in the mood for a revolution,
just a little something so I don't feel gypped.
My passion for you comes from deep within.
I love Eve and her apple... that original sin.

There's a saying I heard a while back:
"Love must be given away or else I lose it."
I believe this... so if I want to keep your love,
I have to share it with others, and God up above.
If I don't, it won't work, and that's the pits.
The same goes for you, my love. That's a fact!
Today I sense that the sharing maybe over,
for your voice, your mannerism is much colder.

Challenges... like waves, must be met at the tip,
the apex, to attain the greatest impact.
We've been floundering on the white caps,
bobbing up and down, searching for something to grasp.
In our struggles, we never attained the knack
to work together, to properly learn the flips.
Somehow, we'd better get our act together
Babe... My love just won't bend any further!

You Burned Your Candle From Both Ends

How could I pay tribute to my dear friend Sara that would be fair and honest? In this poem, I tried to take parts of Sara's life that pertained to me, and write it as I felt it. I'm not sure I succeeded. Sara was a very complex person, a walking contradiction, of which I certainly can identify with. As I review the poem, some of the verses seem a bit disjointed, but that was Sara.

Sara had a profound impact on my life. Her thinking and feelings were so in tune with mine when she was sober. When she was drunk, she reminded me of where I would have been had I continued drinking.

For many years, I watched her combat her demons, to try to deal with unfinished business. One of us would telephone and we'd talk for hours. I know she trusted me. Her plate was overflowing, but to her tribute, she dealt with most of the issues once she put the plug in the jug.

I remember that weekend in Northern Alberta, Sara, when you were on a dry drunk. I confronted you on it. I'll never forget the conversation we had. You were in total denial. That night you started drinking. In all honesty, we lost you for ten years. In that period of time, you nearly destroyed everyone and everything that you loved or loved you. How you survived, I'm not sure. You really were out to kill yourself.

I also remember when you were in recovery, and you telephoned me to come and see you, which I did. We talked for about four hours. You told me many secrets that day. I'm not sure if you drank after that time… I heard stories… but I won't be the one to judge, but what I do know is you tried to right the wrongs you had made. You really tried to put out the flame on one end of the candle. Did you succeed? Only you and your maker truly know.

Thank you, Sara, for your valued friendship. As you know, I'm quite a solitary person, and I don't make friends that easily. Losing you has created a void in my life. God bless you, Sara. Take care of your two loved ones. Keep me in mind from time to time.

You Burned Your Candle From Both Ends

To the beat of a different drummer
you chose to live. Is there any wonder
of the reputation you'd attained?
Some folks made sure to take direct aim
at your faults, knowing you couldn't defend,
for, you burned your candle from both ends.

    Some people talked about you sometimes,
    taking your inventory, adding grime,
    then justifying it as being fine.
    More than one person I took to task.
    They felt vulnerable without their mask.
    Hypocrites! At least if they'd been asked.

Friends don't tell you what you want to hear...
they tell you what you need to hear with no fear.
I admired this quality in you.
You'd not back off...you told me the truth,
yet, to yourself you'd lie and pretend,
causing you to burn your candle from both ends.

    You talked a lot, but left few clues.
    Finding you on distant shores feeling blue...
    I wonder if I really did know you!
    Yet, you brought me much laughter.
    You made me see things weren't a disaster,
    only when I tried to be the master.

Each individual becomes a flame.
A brief moment is ours to lay claim,
to leave our mark on fellow man.
That's called life...then we go back to the land.
You left me a lot of imprints, my friend,
even though you burned your candle from both ends.

When people tried to impose their will
on you, you'd react. There was no real thrill
in following someone else's drills.
That wasn't living. I did the same thing...
I wanted others to take my tunes and sing.
You taught me which melodies to bring.

You sought new experiences to gain
knowledge, which, no doubt, would help you attain
your liberation, the ultimate goal.
Yet, how many times did you sell your soul
to urges and desires on a yen?
You loved to burn your candle from both ends.

When you got into your addictions,
your lifestyle became truly a fiction,
and in your mind, it was total conviction.
At these times, I had so much empathy.
I knew you felt you still had plenty
of resources. Not true! You were on empty.

In life, you have to play the hand you're dealt.
To sum it up, that is your wealth.
To do this was so very difficult,
for often, you didn't like the results.
It was nothing for you to change the trend...
you needed to burn your candle from both ends.

I recall so often your quests,
to change the world without any rest.
You would challenge yourself…a test.
I understood this as part of your illness.
Eventually, you'd rise to your crest,
to find the floodgates open to your abyss.

To me what really is a true crime,
be it written or spoken is: "No Time."
That's exactly what happened to us,
Sara, complacency and laziness.
Would there have been any changes in the end?
I doubt it. You burned your candle from both ends.

My lessons learnt: Enjoy each day.
The years go by so quickly, come what may.
I should count my blessings without delay,
plus, never take them for granted…never…
health and good fortunes maybe severed.
The only thing…Eternity is forever.

Life is not a creation of man,
nor is death. That is all God's plans.
Your leaving has caused a deep void in me,
more than I would've ever thought it to be.
You'll always hold a special place, my friend.
Help me not burn my candle from both ends.

I can still recall the first time we met.
A dizzy blonde who was all in a fret.
Thank you God for the gift that you sent.
Today, all I have are memories
to which I can fall back and flee,
remembering you, knowing you are free.

Life Within a Silence

This poem, extracted from my memory bank of a few years back, gives me a better understanding, today, why I still have a few negative thoughts left to get rid of. Actually, there are quite a few of these thoughts.

I've been hurt a number of times, and there seems to be different degrees of hurt. Because of this I started to put up defenses, keeping my thoughts to myself, drinking to try to put me in a happy mood, to see life on a different angle. Of course, it only got worse, what with all these vices that I figured were the answer. Finally, I reached my crisis... my bottom. Thank God, I look at things on a totally different sphere today.

I have always been one to keep my thoughts to myself. Sure I mouth off and argue a bit, but I enjoy solitude and silence... with background music, a book, a pen and paper to transmit my thoughts, my feelings. Life within a silence means to me today: Listening, absorbing, and weighing the pro's and con's. In other words, have my facts straight, then talk or shut up and listen to the facts. It can also be called the process of maturing. I hope my "Life within a silence" continues to expand and grow each day. That's a near impossibility, but to put in that effort in a constructive way is steps in the right direction.

Life Within a Silence

I spent a lot of time on lost dreams
and so many empty tomorrow's.
Procrastination became my theme.
Sitting back on time that's borrowed,
my life was that of defiance.
A life within a silence.

Darkness lifting. Sunrise soon to besiege.
Tides, a lazy roll, crawling to the beach,
gulls, flying low, in the water they reach…
upward swing, shrieking…to the young they teach.
I hear a small motor in the far distance,
breaking the stillness by the sound it enhances.
Life within a silence.

Walking slowly thru the shifting sand,
Jocks only, my body a bronze tan,
Can of worms and fishing rod in hand,
Smoking a butt, not giving a damn.
In the water, I see a small speck,
The harbor. I feel free, and what the heck.
Life within a silence.

Sky, clear blue, but for a trail of white,
Jack on the hook, tugging, looking for a fight,
Finally I drag it in. What a sight!
Contented, I have my meal for the night.
The cabin nestled amongst the pines,
Sheltered, yet inviting and it's mine.
Life within a silence.

The Dippers and the North Star appear,
leaving its images on the lake, the mirror.
Sprawled, relaxed, without a trace of fear,
sipping my beer. Hell, who knows the year!
Lighting a fire for warmth and food.
What a life! I love the solitude.
　　　Life within a silence.

BRRRING...Goddamn alarm! Shit, already eight.
Dark and snowing. Jesus, winters I hate.
Bitch! I don't give a damn if I'm late.
Crummy job. Probably change at this rate.
Right in the middle of a great dream.
Oh my God...I could just yell and scream.
　　　Life within a silence.

Man, what the hell is it all worth?
In today's society, we are just dwarfs.
I don't need this; I'm leaving on the fourth.
Pack my rags, probably head up north.
Friends; Pukes is more like it...using me.
I help no one unless they help me.
　　　Life within a silence.

Today, I feel well inside, quite content.
On thoughts of the past... I've paid my rent.
Much sorrow, much mistrust my words sent,
leaving few friends and many wounds to mend.
Today, all issues, I like to see the end.
I'm more open, coming out of my den.
　　　Life within a silence.

I'm trying hard to improve my life.
It's difficult…there is much strife…
Then I'm more determined. Onward I strive.
Talk is easy. Often the walk doesn't jive.
Perhaps one way is to set up goals.
That's a wonderful way to soothe the soul.
Life within a silence.

Yes, life can be great within a silence.
I will find the right music to dance,
the right partner to feel some romance,
and, we'll just imagine we're in France.
I'll make sure the alarm clock is broken.
This is too much fun to be awoken!
Life within a silence.

Beautiful, Mystic Feelings

To express a feeling that is felt under extraordinary circumstances is almost unattainable. Almost, I said.

The words in this poem may not have attained the true feelings I felt during this spiritual experience. If I get in the right setting, have an open mind, imagine myself experiencing God's nature, then I too may experience a Beautiful Mystic Feelings again. If not, well, I'll enjoy the poem anyway.

PS: The setting was between Radium Hot Springs and the Village of Radium, during a late fall afternoon. By the time I reached my suite, a storm was raging, and this was the feeling I experienced. I guess I was in the right mood, for it was quite moving.

Beautiful Mystic Feelings

Leaves, the color of rust,
shimmering to the ground.
Skies, brooding darkly,
ready to shed a round.
Mountains, a rocky white,
leaving no trace of brown.
Wind, yelling its rage,
whistling an eerie sound.
  Beautiful Mystic Feelings.

Nights, starting to fall,
darkness envelops me.
Stars, a dullish blue,
seeming only to flee.
Walks, begin to fade,
leaving but mystery.
Lamps, stabbing it's light,
showing me things to see.
  Beautiful Mystic Feelings.

Snow, sadly flaking down,
like tears of guilt... remorse.
Wetness, a dull feeling
on my faces bare pores.
Houses, structures so dim
trees are shading its course.
Bushes, flickering wildly
to the winds strong force.
  Beautiful Mystic Feelings.

Feelings, so passionate,
moved with nature's ways.
Walking and breathing air
so freshly pure...A daze!
Feelings, touching, grabbing
and leading me astray,
unknown but to God,
emotionally I pray.
Beautiful Mystic Feelings.

So Beautiful...So Moving...So Real!

Life's Secrets: To Take Time to...

I was asked to write a poem for Grampa and Winnie's twentieth anniversary. Well, I wrote a poem all right, but I never wrote about them in particular. What I tried to do was place myself in their shoes, and imagine how they would enjoy all the secrets of life. How they would answer the questions with their knowledge and wisdom. Through this thought pattern and imagination, I came up with this poem. In some circles this is called empathy... a very loving experience.

This next paragraph, I read some time ago. I'm not certain the exact words so I can't say it verbatim, therefore I'll paraphrase it. "It takes a long time to find out what is timeless... That being LOVE." We certainly have love here today.

Life's Secrets:
To Take Time to ...

Take time to work; Take time to rest...
At times, life can be a veritable test.
To find this balance, plus make a small nest,
often enough, in life, one must quest,
to attain a goal. The price of success.

Take time to think; Take time to understand...
There may be times you have to take a stand.
To think: The source of power of man.
Look to your soul for the answers...you can!
If you feel right, God'll lend you a hand.

Take time to unwind; Take time to play...
For mental stress, there is no better way.
And physically, what little there's to pay,
all the benefits make for a better day.
It's called the secret of youth...that's what they say!

Take time to learn; Take time to read...
Reading and learning plants the seeds
to help us search and find our needs.
This fountain of knowledge is the key,
to open-mindedness, to let us see.

Take time to worship; Take time to pray...
We must believe in a God, come what may.
Get on your knees and give thanks for today.
Ask Him to guide you and show you the way.
This Higher Power is really okay.

Take time for companions; Take time for friends...
People we trust and don't want to offend.
We enjoy the warm vibes they continue send,
plus, the knowledge, they're willing to lend.
They become a main source of joy in the end.

Take time to Love; Take time for tenderness...
Share your problems, share your happiness.
Show your affection, leave out the stress.
Surrender your love, ask for forgiveness.
This sacrament of life is the very best.

Take time to Imagine; Take time to Dream...
Don't be afraid to create and scheme.
Go to Pluto, Venus, or the Philippines.
Sometimes it's nice to be on a winning team,
but it's not that important. Don't be mean!

Take time to Laugh; Take time to Smile...
Be a jester every once in a while.
This helps with life's tribulations and trials.
Be exuberant! Present a happy style...
It may help that special one the extra mile.

Take time to set Goals; Take time to Plan...
Strive to attain all your desires, and...
enjoy life's pleasures all that you can.
Love your friends...tell them...hold them by the hand,
for, time is of essence, then back to the land.

Take time to be polite; Take time to Revere...
It's so important to respect your peers.
Often, their reflections are in our mirror.
Grandpa and Winnie, you've both been so dear.
I love you! Your presence is always so near.

And, For This I Ask Your Forgiveness

For the past year, Mary has not been well. What with past feelings, the pregnancy, just to name a few problems, she finds life quite difficult. Her health is good. She looks good. Actually, she has most of everything going for her, but obviously not.

In this poem, I'm suggesting a few answers to some of your poignant feelings. Most of the time I know what works for me, and often I try to push this onto you. It causes many problems. I'm not you, Mary. Please forgive me.

I read in "The Treasure Chest," a prose that sums it up best for me: "God asks no man whether he will accept life... this is not the choice. You must take it. The only choice is how!"—My exact feelings. And I do love you.

And, For This, I Ask Your Forgiveness

I ask myself so often lately
the reasons for your unhappiness.
And really, how can I know your ways,
but, I do see and don't have to guess
at how you want control, come what may.
You know no limit. You cannot rest.

My lifestyle didn't believe in moss,
so, I created havoc without a cause.
Looking back, it was a total loss.
I had to go thru a lot of pain
before I let go. I was quite vain.
Today, I let God accept the fame.

I see you try to be so perfect.
You are unforgiving to yourself,
plus, you just won't... let be... to forget.
This is taking a toll on your health.
Off your pretty face sadness deflects,
draining all your assets, your wealth.

I was told: "Try and seek guidance
instead of so much defiance."
"Get approval of your own conscience
rather than the applause of the crowd."
To accept this for someone so proud
was tough. Today it's become a vow.

Often I see you start a project,
knowing that it will not see it's end.
Really, I don't know to what you object,
or why you cannot support your yen.
Fear of failure...therefore you reject?
These are the signals the brain cells send.

I must have a confidence in me,
a belief in my abilities.
Truth, faith, reliance are the key,
to my completing a special task.
Also, I must let go of my past.
All the tools I need, to God I ask.

You dislike yourself with a passion;
therefore, you try to be someone other
than you. You fantasize this put on
as your desire and needs occur.
You are truly an artist. The Con!
Something you sincerely sought after.

My mirror can observe, can perceive,
but alas, it can truly deceive,
lest I know what signals to receive.
I must conduct an introspection,
a detailed self-examination.
To love self is a true sensation.

The past...Work and Action completed,
but not for you... often you return.
I'll find you in some corner seated,
thinking. A true compulsion to yearn,
trying to replenish stock depleted.
Wishful thoughts. There's nothing you can learn.

Of my mental state, I must take care.
It's the only one I've got. It's rare.
Thus, the misfortunes hardest to bear
are those we believe, which never come.
Remembering where this thought comes from
I live for today...I have some fun.

Being unable to cope with stress,
your life has become a severe test.
I see you crying tears of sadness.
My heart, in complete anguish, cries out.
I want to help, but I cause more doubt,
or so it seems. All I do is shout.

Walking unsure down my path of life,
I truly feel someone up above.
I ask for love that I might enjoy life.
I got life that I might enjoy love.
I've made many mistakes in my life.
My inability of your love
being one. I really made a mess,
and, for this, I ask your forgiveness.

The Halloween Costume

I joined a writers' club. I guess it's been going for a year, but I just decided to join this year. Vi, the one who got it going, read some of my poems this past summer, and she convinced me to give it a try... so I did.

Our first meeting was a month ago. It was fine. We were six people of different ages and different "likes." We chatted about the different types of writing we preferred, and what we had done as far as exposure, or merely for our own personal gain. I also found out that there's homework...Yuk! Because I was new and my specialty is poetry, for homework Vi suggested a funny Halloween poem. Well, here is my shining works.

Actually, it was fun to write this. I needed something light for a change, and this certainly fit the bill.

The Halloween Costume

October 31st…the night of goblins and ghosts…
and those big ugly ravens perched on their posts.
The jack-o'-lanterns, peering out of their pumpkin shells,
with triangle eyes and gaping, eerie smiles, trying to tell
us to be wary of those brew makers who screech and yell…
you know… the long nosed, black-frocked creatures from hell,
the broom riders, zig-zagging, showing off, so boastful,
with the full moon portraying their absurdity to the utmost.

On the streets, kids in costumes yelling, "Trick or treat!"
as they run up the front steps. The door opens with a squeak,
as a big monster appears, ready to pounce on his prey.
The poor little folk, stunned by this freak, begin to pray,
Screaming, "Dear God!"; the demon yells, "What did you say?"
One little gaffer repeats, "Trick or Treat? Have a nice day?"
The villain lets go a laugh, "Open your bags for your feast!"
The kids open their gunnysacks, then take a quick retreat.

Out of nowhere, two black people appear in white sheets
Yelling out the mantra, "Trick or treat. Smell my dirty feet."
Mrs. Green comes to the door, sayin', "Who's you tryin' to be?"
"We's in white sheets." "We's angels…can't you see?"
"You's black…no such thing as black angels…not even maybe."
"You's figure som'thun diffrint," she said with a glee.
The young boy and girl, dejected, head down the risky street.
He has an idea. "Come on…this ole gal we're gonna beat."
They yelled, "Trick or Treat…smell my dirty feet!"

117

"Who's you this time?" "We's Billy and Martha Yeats,
the Irish poet." "You's can't be them…They's lily white,"
said Mrs. Green. "We's black folk…so get this right!"
"But why can't we imitate white folk? They ain't so bright."
said the boy. "Find some colored folk who have seen the light."
"Martha"…with her silky blouse and skirt with the pleats,
walked out the door with "Billy." This had become quite a feat.

The young Negro boy thought real hard to figure out a jest.
Pulling off his clothes, he said to his sister, "Get undressed."
"Trick or treat…" Mrs. Green nearly fainted in disbelief.
She sputters out: "Who's you trying to be? A thief?"
The young folks, without a stitch, shivering like a leaf,
look at this older lady and start laughing with relief.
"No! We's two chocolate bars, and we's the best."
"One with nuts and one without. Wanna check to guess?"

One old cackling witch, trying to abscond her vulgar ways,
notice the young couple in the nude, performing their charade.
Zooming in for a closer look, she nearly fell off her broom.
Noticing their clothes on the road scattered and strewn,
she looks around, slowly she turns and down she swoons
to pick them up. It's really, really cold… minus 20, full moon.
Landing right beside them, she hands them a hot coffee
and their garments. Mrs. Green lost it. She went crazy,
ranting and screaming about that grace that was amazing.

Self Portrait
(Thru the eyes of others)

This is a different type of poem. I'm trying to see me through the eyes of different people that I know, to imagine what they really think of me.

What I have written in these verses are very real in my mind's eyes, for I felt them before, and I still feel them.

I thank the many, many people involved in this small search of myself. It's another way for me to gain a bit of insight, to try and 'better' my own self-portrait. I'm not sure that 'better' is the right word... 'understand' is probably more accurate; and from there I can change if I see fit.

To my brother and sisters... thank you for your feelings displayed, for it shows you think and worry about me.

Self Portrait
(Thru the eyes of others)

Thru the eyes of acquaintances

He seems like a happy-go-lucky guy.
To worry about tomorrow, he says "Why?"
A partying man, he goes to the end.
He likes to tell jokes, laughter he sends.
He's not the type to be taken serious,
he don't give a shit, he ain't curious.
A real neat guy to know, hell, who knows,
someday to another party we may go.

Thru the eyes of colleagues

For a certain few, man, you're out of luck,
for he just won't accept, "To pass the buck."
He doesn't walk into something blind.
Also, he's not afraid to speak his mind.
He's no sloucher, plus he won't take the fall,
he always tries his very best…that's all.
Don't criticize him unless you're right,
because he'll get mad and very uptight.

Thru the eyes of true friends.

Boy, he sure does enjoy drinking a lot.
For his good, maybe he should try to stop.
He honestly doesn't know his limits,
which is too bad, he always goes the limit.
He's a happy, friendly sort of guy,
to lend a hand, he will certainly try.
He enjoys meeting people, in general,
but, he dislikes very much betrayals.

Thru the eyes of lovers

He's not bad looking, or so it seems,
but, on companionship, he tends to lean.
He always seems to produce a good line,
but contradictory and moody at times…
Quite hard to please, not much composure,
yet, willing to offer someone his shoulder.
To have to commit to only one person,
would not work. A taboo, for certain!

Thru the eyes of my parents

He has a wonderful personality,
but often forgets about realities.
He's quite smart, a good intelligence,
but wasting it, it seems, with a vengeance.
He has a huge problem with liquor.
We try not, but we always seem to bicker.
It would be very nice, if he settled down.
Certainly, would cause less worry and frown.

Thru the eyes of siblings.

Always in the process of making an ass
of himself. So frustrating, just no class.
It would be nice if he'd find a good woman,
instead of all the tramps he seems to tend.
Alcohol, not a doubt, his biggest problem,
but, no helping hand does he want us to lend.
It'd be good to see him in his old ways,
instead of his reclusive ways, today.

Thru the eyes of self

I thank you all for your grateful thoughts,
and a very good lesson I've been taught.
Each of you is right in your own minds,
but I'm not so sure that I'm right in mine.
Everything that was said, is part of me,
and, I ask, "Is that the way it's supposed to be?"
Looking over all these different remarks,
with some help, I may step out of the dark.
Also, I realize…I'm only human!!

Hamburg's Mist

Listening to Radio Luxembourg, I heard "Kentucky Rain" by Elvis. It inspired me to write this poem.

This Hamburg Mist is a happening late at night/early morning because of the climate. Unfortunately, my job starts at 6:00am, therefore, I'm up and gone by 5:00am. I have to walk about fifteen minutes before I catch the U-Bahn, so I'm in this fog, literally, most everyday.

Often, I feel totally engulfed in this mist. I imagine my sweetheart walking beside me. We talk. I try to guide and counsel her in her choices. She has the looks and body of a model.

In my mind, I feel she's listening, but is she following my advice? And, really, who am I to give out advice, and why should she follow it? She has her own mind and opinions... but the mist doesn't project this... merely positive pictures.

To mention: Hamburg has one of the biggest Red Light Districts in all of Europe, being a seaport city. St. Paulii is very well renowned.

A note: We broke up while I was in Hamburg, and not long after, she met someone and was married. I saw her a few years back. She is now divorced. When I think of that period of my life, I have really changed. At that time, I was totally out of control with alcohol. To prove to myself I didn't have a problem, I needed "Power Over" someone. Rachel fit that bill to a T. What a crock... I often mused of what would have happened if I had treated her with respect. I know she loved me. She was as honest as I was dishonest. She is still a very beautiful woman. The time I saw her, I made my amends to her. She was pleased. She also reminded me of how much of a jerk I really was at that time. She certainly was right.

Hamburg's Mist

Hamburg's Mist, you impenetrable whore,
so powerful, so mighty, and so true.
In your cover of guilt and deception,
why leave the negatives that you do?

The river Elbe, very majestic-like,
flows swiftly, yet so lonely...by and by.
Its body is full of sorrow and hate,
we need not have to ask the whys.

Off this river comes a creeping mist,
dulling the many bright lights that glare.
And in this disguise, I really see
a beautiful person for whom I care.

The thoughts I have in this snowy blanket,
leave me with pure happiness...I'm content.
The imprints left on my mind are so dear,
I won't share. They cannot be bought or lent.

Imagining you in this cloak, this carpet,
I see a person for whom I can hold,
someone who truly wants to be with me,
on one condition. You want to keep your soul.

As the sun stretches, then rises,
your comely picture begins to fade.
"Don't go!" I'm saying, as my open hand
grasps at the photo my mind has laid.

Light brown hair with a dimpled chin,
twinkling eyes…a slight smile…so true.
A beautiful woman floating away.
I let out a sigh. I feel down, I feel blue.

Hamburg's Mist, you impenetrable whore,
so powerful, so mighty, so true.
In your cover of guilt and deception,
why leave the negatives that you do?

All day long, I think of these moments,
anticipating these mind photos again.
As the night starts to inch it's way in,
the agent hobbles slowly from its bend.

Slowly walking late at night, pondering,
my body becomes covered with you,
for already, the river has released
its valve, sending its mist so very true…

I'm Kinda Wondering...

When I read or hear how women are treated in a majority of the countries in the world, I really shudder. In some places animals have more rights than a woman... How can that be? It's been said to me "well that's their culture." It still isn't right. We take it that in our own country, women are often treated "less than"... and, again I ask myself why? All the old clichés come to surface: "man is the stronger sex", "it's a male dominant society", "it's society's fault that women are portrayed as such", and the list goes on.

This poem was written concerning marriages. A lot of the women whom I've talked to, often feel "less than." The majority feels that perhaps they brought this attitude with them into the relationship. Why? Teachings of their parents, teaching of their schools/teachers—the limitations and expectations were "less than" of men's—teachings of their peers, teachings of their jobs—lower paying, more menial—the teachings of society.

Therefore, starting out in a relationship feeling this way without realizing it... usually subconsciously, they bring this aura with them. Often, men have preyed on this attitude, certainly feeling its presence. The women, on the other hand, want to be treated equal, even though this stigma is still present. Then the problems begin... and often end in a divorce.

I have no solutions to this dilemma, other than I make an effort to treat everyone equal, and, often that's not an easy task. If others do the same, and many do, then society is changing for the better.

I'm Kinda Wondering...

Why do I sense so much angst,
so much apprehension of your thoughts?
It would be nice to hear... "thanks...
you are very special... you do a lot.
You're honest. I appreciate
how you tell it to me straight."
I often muse...how long before I go...
before you show me the open gate.
I'm kinda wondering...
will you still want me tomorrow?

       What will tomorrow bring me?... I'm not sure...
       Why do I feel so unworthy, so insecure?
       Is it because of all my childhood baggage...
       things that happened which I couldn't gauge?
       Honest, I had no control, no way to steer
       all the crap I received, including my fears.
       Parents hurt me emotionally, and I strayed...
       couldn't fulfill their wants, so good-by, I bade.

Each time I tell you my feelings,
You just turn and walk away.
I'm so confused ... my mind's a reeling...
wondering "what the heck did I say?"
I observe your demeanor with disquiet...
how you glare right through me. I'll bet
you wish someone else was in this gown...
I can imagine your sobriquets.
I'm kinda wondering...
how much longer I'll be around.

I met many "losers" I felt were "winners."
For some reason, I seem to attract users.
My fears paralyze my thoughts...I took forever
to finally understand. Life's a good teacher.
Over time I've forgiven my mother and father,
but certainly not forgot. Often I conjure
back to my past. Some of the memories have faded,
yet, there are some that still make me afraid.

At the beginning, you were so sensitive.
I loved your distinctive attention.
You have a gift...You were so perceptive,
missing nothing. By the way, did I mention...
you always deemed me so special,
which, for me, was quite unusual.
You never asked about my past...
In your eyes, nothing seemed questionable.
So, I'm kinda wondering...
What happened? Nothing appears to last.

I was very naive and trusting...so insecure.
Becoming a follower certainly was my cure.
This remedy allowed me to fit right in.
The morals were loose...we cared not about sin.
I'd accepted this freedom as part of my rights...
I had cowered enough...I learnt how to fight
to keep this independence. I loved this taste...
this life...no obligations. Time was in no haste.

The law states that women are equal,
then why do I feel so inferior?
Like a mercenary, I'm quite venal.
The label brands me as a whore...
My past is slapping me in the face,
leaving all sorts of tracks and traces.
When women do things, they're a sleaze,
yet, when men do it, they get praise!
I'm kinda wondering...
How long before you ask for my keys.

    The first time I met you, I felt a desire,
    a real need. Your presence ignited this fire.
    All the others were from a different weave...
    Your texture, your character I could believe,
    which made me happy. I loved you unequivocally.
    To hope for the same in return, indeed was a folly.
    I've come to the conclusion that it must be me...
    my looks, my acts, my manners...my personality.

Why do we always hurt the ones
we love? Perhaps a transference...
those reactions that cause the passion
to erupt at the loved one's expense?
Whatever the reason, it still hurts.
Many times, I become quite irked...
Why? Often I feel very alone...
in your presence. So little comfort.
Consequently, I'm kinda wondering...
How long this is going to be my home.

My gift to you is who I am, what I believe in...
What you give in return is your stoicism.
Lately your thoughts have been easy to discern,
my sole role...I am the vessel for your sperm.
I imagined we were to share our reflections,
by talking about recollections and retrospections.
I may have low self-esteems, but I'm worth more...
a lot more... The writing's on the wall, what's in store.

In our lifetime, come what may,
we'll be judged by our criterion
of life... that of our journey,
not of our ego...the godless felon.
Also, wealth doesn't buy happiness,
as our union depicts, just more stress...
I want us to stay together...
Can we change or continue to regress?
I'm kinda wondering...today...
because all I perceive is a shiver.

Sometimes "life" plays the odd dirty trick,
then sits back while I take my licks.
I'm kinda curious where God was through this.
I don't recall feeling much of His bliss...
but, I sure felt loneliness and lots of sadness.
We certainly are both to blame for this mess.
I'm strong enough to get through your neglect...
with God's help. He'll guide me and protect...
You must decide what the outcome will bring.
And so...I'm kinda wondering...

The Professional at Work

In this poem, I can identify with everything that was written. It could very well be me. I was lucky, I never reached the type of low that the character in this poem did, but I still reached my low. Being an alcoholic, I understand fully well that alcohol is very destructive.

This poem has many different characters, but the one I thought and used the most is anonymous. Still today, I often wonder whatever became of him. It would not surprise me to hear that he's dead. At the same time, I wouldn't care what the autopsy would say, I know that alcohol would be the major reason for his death. If nothing else, you are helping me stay sober...one day at a time...Thanks.

The Professional at Work

For someone who could walk so tall,
seeing him stumble, stagger, and crawl,
nearly does bring tears to my eyes.
This act is showing me he's not so wise,
even though he's still trying to disguise.
Everyone knows, yet he still denies.

    Contradictions is the game he plays,
    crying for help, saying stay away.
    Mad no one came, the old pot he stirs,
    unleashing past, forgotten treasures.
    He's getting even by dispelling hurt.
    Uncorking the bottle, with death he flirts.
    Notice please, the professional at work.

He was a dreamer, a real schemer,
a true master…when the needs occurred.
He could set you up with a quick glance,
by analyzing your body, your stance.
He'd know what plan to set in motion,
to con you, to play on your emotions.

Taking everyone's inventory,
was his specialty. He need not worry.
But, to question himself, are you kidding?
No way! That he could have been fibbing?
Impossible. Others were to blame.
How could anyone dare tarnish his name.

And, of course, the booze is always present.
Everything else, clothes, food, and the rent,
are the last items on this very short list
of needs. Addicted, he must persist
in nourishing his habit, his crutch.
With time, this also becomes way too much.

By now, people are wizened to his ways.
He's losing his touch, more and more each day.
His only thoughts are how to buy more booze,
so back to the street. There's nothing to lose.
Finally, one day, he looks in the mirror...
What's he see? Worry, resentment, and fear.

It's hard to imagine, or so it seems,
how fast he's attained these destructive means.
Please tell me. How do you measure time?
Perhaps, the sand in the glass is the sign?
Or, could it be the distance that he'll climb,
on that jagged road, to his box of pine?

The passion, the motivation, the pain,
have caught up to him. Crying out in vain,
he shows us a glimpse of his true self.
But, it's too late. And now, even his health
is not good. His eyes are vacant, dreamless,
like old stained windows. He's in a real mess.

At last, he achieved his point of no return.
Now, about all he can do is yearn
of a past he's really never had.
The alcohol made it so, and that is sad.
Always alone, no one with to confide,
only his bottle. He seeks places to hide.

He senses something is just not right,
even his best friend has lost its might.
Knowing that his time is near, he's terrified.
His life flashes past. What a downhill slide!
What a ride! He doesn't believe in heaven,
yet, he's praying that hell won't be his haven.

How do you have empathy for someone,
who all his life abused, was such a bum?
Are we to judge? There's a lesson to be taught
for all of us. I can use the food for thought.
There's a bit of good…and bad in all of us.
Be thankful to the One. It is only just.

Contradictions are the game he plays.
Crying for help, saying stay away.
Mad no one came, the old pot he stirs,
unleashing past, forgotten treasures.
He's getting even by dispelling hurt.
Uncorking the bottle, with death he flirts.
Notice please, the professional at work.

Tom Was my Friend

I needed to write a poem attributing it to my friend Tom. It just seemed so fitting. From the first time I met him until the last time I saw him, not many days before he died, Tom was one of the most considerate persons that I have ever met. He really did think of everyone's best interest before undertaking a project for himself.

By the time I met Tom, he'd taken an early retirement, and he was into the handyman status. He loved carpentry, and he certainly was knowledgeable about this trade. He did a lot of work for us, our family, in repairs and construction.

Tom was a diplomatic person. He knew the right words for the situation. Tom was assertive, as I am aggressive. He worked more with his thoughts than emotions. He knew how to respond, where I know how to react. I haven't changed much, but at least I know that if and when the day will come for me to change, I can use Tom's example as a guide. I loved watching him at meetings. He had a distinct way of asking questions without stepping on anybody's toes.

I considered Tom my friend. He always respected my opinion. He always made me feel good. He was great to be around. I miss you Tom... You take care of Madelaine, Tommy, Diane, and Harold. I know you will, plus you'll do the same for the in-laws and your grandchildren. You were lucky to have them in your life, but they were so fortunate to have you in their lives. God bless and take care.

Tom Was my Friend

When a man starts constructing his new home,
a level, solid foundation is a must.
Having done this, he knows that he can trust
his wish of adding mortar and stone.
Having the blueprints implanted on his brain,
he's aware that if things go wrong, he's to blame.

My friend, Tom, was such a kind person.
He wasn't impressed by people's cursin'.
He could accomplish so much, for the credit
didn't matter to him. He had so much wit,
and when challenged he'd light up in total bliss.
A man of much wisdom, life had taught him this.

Leveling and laying the footing forms,
the carpenter proceeds to pour cement.
Next come the walls for the basement,
and a cement floor, in case of heavy storms.
Weeping tiles are needed for drainage,
as is tar on the walls to stop seepage.

Tom always made you feel quite comfortable
at his home, when you sat around his table.
I liked his quiet, yet determined ways.
He liked to be centered, his shade was gray.
Tom was well organized and not one to quit.
He knew what he wanted to do, then did it.

Having completed pouring the basement,
he moves on to the framing and the floor.
It's all falling into place. The 2 x 4's,
plywood, rafters, beams, and window casements,
held together with nails, screws, and glue.
It's coming along good...To date no rue.

Tom was very good with measures and angles,
so length and widths he could well handle.
The height of my friends accomplishments
always equaled the depth of what he meant...
his credence, his beliefs, his convictions.
One nice thing, Tom always had clear diction.

Putting the shingles on the roof is the next step,
and covering the outer wood to protect
from nature's elements or they'd be wrecked.
Bricks and siding are used to stop this wet.
It's time for windows and doors to be installed
in their allotted locations in the walls.

On take-off, an airplane goes against the wind,
not with it. When things went wrong, he'd bear and grin,
knowing he wasn't the one who was insane,
even though he had bucked the system...in vain.
When need be, Tom's displays were quite dynamic,
and when issues didn't mesh, he didn't panic.

To make sure that his thoughts and feelings
are on the same page, he consults his blue prints.
Now is the time to make sure there is no dint
in his plans. No more wheeling and dealing.
It's time to measure and frame each room,
so then the trades people can come very soon.

Tom was a good delegator, he knew
who could do what. When he had himself a crew,
it was similar to his life…stimulating…
full of action, certainly not diminishing.
Tom tried to live in the moment, and most times
he succeeded. His choices were always in rhyme.

With the electrical wiring, the gas line,
the furnace, with its hot and cold air ducts,
the water and sewer lines all hooked up,
the inspector is happy. That's a good sign!
It's now time to insulate, then either gyproc,
panel or both. To clear his mind, he takes a walk.

Tom was truly a dedicated family man,
and if his neighbor needed a lending hand
it was there. He loved his wife with a passion,
and his kids he adored without question.
The twinkle in his eye was his grand children.
They trusted him. He was their greatest friend.

The design chosen for the walls and ceilings
are quite unique with the colors sand/coral.
The cupboards and shelves fit this match very well.
This style gives off so much warmth and feelings,
encouraged by the choice of rugs and tiles.
Looking at his work, the man feels pride…he smiles.

Tom's point of view was always held in respect,
at the workshops and committees, he did trek.
His attitude was actually quite simple...
"It's better to defeat me on principle,
than to win by cheating and telling me lies."
Tom was in tune with self. He hated disguises.

Completing all of the trim and the base boards,
it's time to put up the curtains and blinds.
The contrasting shams, which were hard to find...
so rich and alluring, plus he could afford.
The end is near...it seems that it took forever.
What an accomplishment, what an endeavor.

Tom was my friend, and that means a lot to me.
He treated me with respect, plus he helped me see
many different aspects, and some of the choices
that I had. Tom strongly encouraged me to voice
my opinions, and if they happened to be wrong,
to learn the reasons why. Now my friend is gone.

It took quite a while to finally finish...
moving all the dirt for the landscaping,
planting trees, grass, ponds, flowers... everything!
What a grand success...so homey... so rich,
notably with the unique flowing little stream.
He's attained the realities of his dreams.

"I'm going to give Tom a call so he can fix
that door again! He'll need his bag of tricks."
I can't do that anymore...my friend's left us...
he's met his Maker, the carpenter's son, Jesus.
My! Heaven's a better place with his presence.
So long my friend. I miss your wit, your common sense,
but I really miss not seeing you. That's the essence.

The Ultimate Pain of Love

This was not the poem I wanted to write, but I guess it must have been... for here it is.

I had every intention of writing a poem on the stupidity of our Federal Government talking about decriminalizing marijuana. For many people that would be fine, but for a whole lot of people it would just open the door to full-fledged drugs... and where does it end...? If one type is legal, before long many more types are legal. Instead of prevention, it's permission. I understand the governments thinking... there's a LOT of MONEY to be had, and morals mean nothing, and for those who are or become addicted...who cares! A lot will kill themselves off, some will be put in prisons for all sorts of crimes, and the few that make it to rehab and a few social/drug addiction programs, that's fine. Hell, the money made by them being the buyer, distributor, and wholesaler, will be WAY MORE than the costs of jail or a few coffins or a few social programs. I hate to see what will happen when this all takes place. I may still write a poem on this issue.

This poem may have happened to someone the way I wrote it...I don't know, but I've heard of similar situations, and it's sad... sad to be caught up in the addiction and have no way out. You may say, "There are lots of ways out." You're right, but for people like the guy in the poem, they are mentally sick human beings, and they are incapable of grasping a way out, and fear is the main catalyst... to have to live life without this crutch, this friend... there's no possible way.

Now, while this person is intent on killing himself or herself, family and friends don't understand...they are on the other side of the equation. As a parent, to have to see my son literally kill himself, and there is absolutely nothing I can do... some part of me would also die. Love is such a strong emotion... the strongest... and the strongest feeling of this emotion is our children. The pain of birth is joyous... we share with many, but the pain of death is sadness... we grieve alone. Both these pains are the ultimate pain of love.

The Ultimate Pain of Love

When the fetus decides to become part of the world,
it makes its presence known by forcing and shoving.
The mother feels paroxysm she's never felt before,
but these throes are a positive pain... a birth...
and, it was well worth it... The ultimate pain of love.

Life was fine for this young fellow...he was smart,
good-looking, lots of friends, a flair for art...
A quick observation... he had a real good start
if he wanted success, but first he had to part
with some of his friends, some real good con-arts.
Being a follower... he just didn't have the heart.

The pipe organ's sound resonates throughout
the church, echoing feelings of despondency.
Grief and anguish are very prevalent, very dominant.
You could hear the pain, you could feel the pain...
So much sorrow in the tragic loss of this loved one.

At first, it was the thrill of maybe being caught.
hell, it wasn't too alarming, just a little pot,
but, before too long, more serious drugs were sought.
School became the milieu where narcotics were bought.
In a very short time, he was hooked. His "friends" taught
him brisk money. Drugs and goods that were hot.

The minister enters from his sacristy, proceeds
behind the casket and sincerely welcomes everyone.
He talks of the young man lying in front of him...
not condemning, not condoning... simply explaining
the hard road chosen and the resulting consequences.

The home life... he left... had become too unbearable.
His parents felt guilt and shame. They felt terrible.
It was beyond their comprehension... They were unable
to grasp his sickness, so they believed his fables...
they had to. To deal with truth, they weren't able...
therefore, through it all they continued to enable.

He also talks of feelings and forgiveness,
explaining that the young man wasn't a bad person,
no... he was an emotionally sick human being.
Now, God was treating and taking special care of him
through His encompassing, compassionate love.

For a few weeks, he took advantage of friends,
but, that didn't last long... on the streets he ends.
He's new to this style of life, so he follows the trends.
Soon he's hustling like the rest. No more pretends...
He's now part of the culture. The money he spends,
bottle picking and welfare, are for the drugs of his yen.

Swinging open the big oak doors of the church,
slowly, the attendants guide the coffin to the steps.
Each pallbearer, friends of the deceased, pick-up
their chum, carefully bring him to the waiting hearse.
Of all the joy rides he'd taken, this will be the shortest.

He needs more money... his addiction demands it.
The pushers and dealers weren't giving out credit,
therefore, he started stealing... he had to have his hit.
He's now started mainlining... life's become a conflict,
in his heart knowing it's wrong, yet not able to quit.
What a dilemma, he feels like a piece of shit.

Following close behind, the immediate family
make their presence felt through muffled sobs.
Heads bowed, the tears slowly creep down their cheeks,
they huddle close together, supporting one other.
None can understand why it had come to this.

Ending up in a hospital, after an overdose,
he was sent to a rehab to deal with his ghosts.
Afraid to check his closets, he decides to coast.
Not pleased with looking at self, he starts to boast
of his exciting life. Wanting his counselor to toast
his wise ways, he's disappointed with his hosts.

As the hearse door closes, the driver patiently waits
for the grieving people to enter the courtesy cars.
Headlights shining, taking turns to get in line,
the procession begins. The line of cars is long.
Passing motorists show respect by pulling over.

Even though he OD'd, he felt in good health...
he felt invincible... real denial... lying to self.
Back in familiar surroundings he finds himself...
in the slums. Sadness, yet comfort is what he felt.
Tracking down his comrades, he needs some wealth,
for, he's not happy with the crap being dealt.

Reaching the gravesite, the driver heads for
the mound of fresh dirt. The carriers place
the coffin on the straps, braced over the hole.
The minister, missal in hand, reads a passage
on how we return to the ground, "Ashes to Ashes..."

Ah! to capture a moment in time before it's too late...
but late it was. He had way too much on his plate.
His body was something a pincushion could relate.
Injecting a needle on most days, he rarely ate.
Sometimes his illusions promised to go straight.
Untrue!...His demons wouldn't allow it...He was afraid.

The physical body is lowered into the ground...
his soul has begun its eternal, spiritual quest.
The ones left behind are still no further ahead...
in fact, their grief has gotten worse...He's gone forever...
they never had the chance to say a proper good-bye.

His family, through contacts, heard of his plight.
Heading to the skids, they found him that night,
unconscious in a fetid squalid room. What a sight!
Off to the hospital... again...stretchers and bright lights,
hoping they'd made it on time. A few felt contrite,
feeling fault, feeling sorrow if he died this night.

Each, in their unique way, expresses their love.
For some it's through anger, for others it's through fear,
and yet others will ask his forgiveness for suffering
they may have caused him. None will understand the whys...
why he'd chosen this lifestyle? Why he had to die?

Upon release, he'd pretty much given up on hope.
Not wanting to live, he pulls out a piece of rope...
yet afraid to die...he reflects and lights a smoke.
His decisions...if he did...family would cry and mope...
and that's life...but if he didn't how would he cope?
Friends found his body hanging...He had choked.

Entering the cold cemented room, sensing death,
a trembling sensation washes over the couple
as the draped corpse is wheeled into the room.
Pulling back the sheet, pain they'd never, ever felt
stabbed them in places they didn't know existed.
Their son lay on the slab. The ultimate pain of love.

Sorrow...you deal with alone...and that's a tough one.
There are times when love cannot change someone...
and this was one of those times. His compulsions,
when drug induced, took away his compunction,
his scruples. In the end, he was left with none.
He had become a prisoner of his own misfortunes.

In looking back on this man's life, it was similar to
a play with many acts. Some of the characters were evil,
some good, some stayed short periods, some longer.
Each and everyone contributed to his disposition.
He had choices...unfortunately he made the wrong ones...
When he came into this world, he came with nothing,
and when he left, he left the same way...with nothing.
It's between these two extremes, he will be judged.

Printed in the United States
17234LVS00001B/130-150